Drills and Exercises in English Pronunciation

STRESS *and* INTONATION

Part 1

Prepared by **ENGLISH LANGUAGE SERVICES, INC.**

Washington, D.C.

COLLIER MACMILLAN INTERNATIONAL
A Division of Macmillan Publishing Co., Inc.
New York

COLLIER MACMILLAN PUBLISHERS
London

Collier Macmillan International
A Division of Macmillan Publishing Co., Inc.
866 Third Avenue, New York, New York 10022
Collier Macmillan Canada, Ltd., Don Mills, Ontario

Printed in the United States of America
20 19 18 17 16

PREFACE

This book and its companion volume, *Stress and Intonation, Part 2*, together with *Consonants and Vowels*, constitute a series of three drill books in English pronunciation with the overall title *Drills and Exercises in English Pronunciation*. All three books are accompanied by pre-recorded tapes, and American pronunciation is exemplified throughout.

Drills and Exercises in English Pronunciation is intended for secondary school or adult students who are learning English. The material in this series is suitable for use as a special course or as a supplement to a basic language program. The drills and exercises are not graded as to difficulty; depending on need, they can be assigned for work at elementary, intermediate, or advanced levels of proficiency. The contents of the three books are so organized that the teacher (or the student pursuing an independent course of study) has convenient access to specific problem areas encountered in the English sound system.

The material in this book is mainly devoted to giving practice and drill on word stress, including noun compounds, and word combination stress; that is, on the characteristic stress rhythm patterns that occur when words in various classes come together: adjective and noun, noun and verb, etc. *Stress and Intonation, Part 2*, is concerned with the placement of the sentence or phrase stress in both contrastive and non-contrastive (non-emphatic or "neutral") situations. Various intonation patterns are introduced in the drill books. An abundance of drill material is included, but the treatment of the features of stress and intonation cannot claim to be exhaustive in that all possible phenomena in spoken English will be found exemplified. The two drill books may be used independently or consecutively.

The introductory statement entitled "Study of Stress, Intonation, and Juncture" outlines in some detail, mainly for teachers, the premises upon which the drill books were constructed and the frame used for presenting the drill material.

Drills and Exercises in English Pronunciation is one of a series of materials in English as a second language created for the Collier-Macmillan English Program by the Materials Development Staff of English Language Services, under the co-direction of Edwin T. Cornelius, Jr., and Willard D. Sheeler. The author of *Stress and Intonation, Part 1*, Willard D. Sheeler, expresses his appreciation to Dr. Kenneth Croft for reading the manuscript and offering comments before publication, and to Earle W. Brockman for his similar contribution and for his assistance with "Study of Stress, Intonation, and Juncture."

TABLE OF CONTENTS

STUDY OF STRESS, INTONATION, AND JUNCTURE

General Observations

A person who, let us say, understands French, can enter a crowded bus in New York and, amid the general babble of English among the passengers, recognize that the people three rows back are speaking French, even though he may not actually overhear any single word clearly enough to say what the people are talking about. If asked how he could identify the language without hearing any words, he would probably say, "Well, it just *sounded* like French; I'm sure that's the language they were speaking."

Why did it sound like French? It sounded that way because French, like all languages, has its own distinctive melodies and rhythms, based on its intonation and stress patterns. Its sentences end on certain characteristic "tunes," or sequences of pitches; its words and phrases follow each other according to certain rhythmic stress patterns and certain arrangements of loud and soft syllables.

The lesson for learners of English—or any language—is that the intonation and stress patterns of the new language are just as important as the sounds of the vowels and consonants. It is just as necessary for the learner to achieve mastery of stress and intonation, as it is for him to say each individual word properly, not only so that hearers can understand him, but so that he can understand what he hears.

Word Stress and Sentence Stress

Both the word stress and the sentence stress must be properly placed if reliable communication is to take place. Everybody knows that English has word stress, and all students with any pretensions whatever to a speaking knowledge of English have been trained to say individual words properly. But there are stress patterns that go beyond the word level. If the student says "He sees IT," for instance, rather than the normal "He SEES it," understanding will be difficult or perhaps, in the case of an unsophisticated listener, impossible.

It may be that the stress system does not bear as great a functional load as other parts of the phonological system do. That is to say, stress, while unquestionably phonemic (since it is not predictable), is usually not quite so critical to meaning as certain other features are. For instance, the difference between a properly stressed word (intélligible) and an improperly stressed one (intelligíble) is most often the difference between a proper English item and a non-existent one, rather than the difference between two possible items (ínvalid, inválid).

Improper mastery of stress and intonation contributes greatly to a "foreign accent" in English. The way that stress is used, and particularly the rhythm of the syllables and the various intonation contours, are of primary importance in giving English its characteristic sound.

Stress is extremely important in signaling syntactic relationships in English. An outstanding example is the matter of noun compounding, and the learner should develop good control of phenomena like the difference between *black bird* (a bird that is black, of whatever species) and *blackbird* (one of the species that is so called, of whatever color—perhaps a newly hatched chick or even an albino specimen that happens to be white). Either word in the expression *black bird* can bear the primary stress, depending on the context. Neutral: *I saw a large black bird.* Contrastive: *I saw a bláck bird, not a brówn one.* The word referring to the species, *bláckbird*, must always have the primary stress on the first syllable, while the second syllable has reduced stress (tertiary in most people's speech, occasionally secondary). There is no choice here; *bláckbird* is an inseparable compound, not an adjective-noun combination or phrase. Example:

> I saw a black bird, but it wasn't a bláckbird.
> Not all black birds are bláckbirds.

Intonation contours have meanings, of course, though it is not always easy to state exactly what these meanings are. Many observers are convinced that babies learn intonation contours before they learn anything else in language, and dogs often seem to respond to intonation rather than to individual words. We can tell from the intonation whether a speaker is asking a yes-no question or making a statement *(They're here.* vs. *They're here?)*; whether he has completed his statement, or whether there is more to come; whether he is stating something categorically, with assurance, or whether he is doubtful, hesitant, seeking corroboration; and whether he is expressing impatience, disgust, or exasperation.

Stress and intonation not always emphasized in English study

Although it is obvious to all language teaching experts today that the foreign learner must be able to use and properly respond to the features of stress and intonation if he is to be fully successful in his mastery of English, it is a fact that the teaching of stress and intonation occupies a subordinate place in a great many classrooms. These features are simply not taught with the same thoroughness, or given the same systematic treatment, as the consonants and vowels. Some of the reasons for this are quite obvious, some less so.

As every teacher knows, the English writing system, aside from the few unreliable clues furnished by the punctuation and the occasional use of special type to represent emphasis, does not represent stress or intonation in any way at all. In order to represent these features, additional markings are needed over and above the regular orthography. Since most text materials are printed in ordinary orthography, neither the teacher nor the student can count on much guidance from them, insofar as stress and intonation are concerned. Not only are intonation and stress markings difficult and expensive to print, but they also clutter up the page with markings that the student does not recognize as English, has to have special training in interpreting, and is likely to resent as an intrusion when he is already faced with the difficult task of learning to read a foreign language.

Another reason for the lack of emphasis on stress and intonation in many classes is that the teacher has not had the opportunity to become acquainted with an analysis or description of these phenomena in scientific terms. It is difficult to deal with intonation (stress is a bit easier, but not much). Describing an intonation contour in words is just about as difficult as describing a melody without actually singing it. A musician can write it out in notes, which another musician can look at and understand, but a person not specially trained in music, even though he might be able to sing a melody perfectly, could never describe it to another person in such a way that the other person could also sing it. He could only say, "It sounds like this," sing the tune, and then have the other person imitate it. This is the way intonation is handled in most instances, of course. The teacher, in common with all speakers of English, uses and responds to the stress and intonation systems completely, with all their subtleties (subject to the peculiarities of dialect), but with most speakers these features function below the "level of awareness", as the anthropologists say. By this we mean that these things operate without conscious choice or deliberate manipulation by the speaker; the speaker says something in a certain way, not because he chooses to say it that way, but simply because "that's the way to say it." Not many speakers, unless they have had special linguistic training, have any objective knowledge of intonation and stress phenomena, other than the obvious matter of the correct placement of word stress. They may be aware that punctuation changes the "tone of voice" in some way, but that is about all. On the other hand, almost all educated speakers are very much aware of consonants and vowels and have usually paid them a great deal of attention (however unscientifically in many cases) in connection with learning to read and spell.

Teachers deal with stress and intonation in various ways

Despite what has just been said, stress and intonation are widely taught. Since it is impossible to say anything in English without stress and intonation, the use of the live, spoken language automatically involves the use of these features. No matter what the model is (live teacher, tape, etc.), the student is given specimens of stress and intonation features for imitation, along with the vowels and consonants and grammatical patterns. This kind of learning through exposure and imitation is normally found in classrooms using the oral-aural method. In the hands of experienced and knowledgeable teachers, this is undoubtedly the best way to teach stress and intonation.

If a generalization is at all possible, it appears that in teaching stress, attention is almost universally paid to two important features: word stress and sentence stress.

Rare is the teacher, however inexperienced, who does not make corrections in these two areas of pronunciation from the first day onwards. Most vocabularies and dictionaries, too, indicate word stress as a matter of course. With regard to intonation, those who teach it usually single out two patterns without fail: the declarative sentence pattern, which is identical with the question-word question pattern *(He's here, What's your name?)*, and the yes-no question pattern, with rising intonation *(Is he here?)*. This is about as far as most textbooks go, however.

Purpose of these materials

It is the purpose of *Stress and Intonation, Parts 1 and 2* to provide a great deal more drill than is usually made available and to treat aspects of both stress and intonation that are not usually covered in conventional English courses. Part 1 concentrates on word stress and on what might be called "word-combination" stress; that is, on the characteristic stress rhythm patterns that occur when words of various classes come together, such as adjective and noun, noun and verb, verb and adverb, etc. Part 2 is concerned with phrase or sentence stress, in both contrastive and non-contrastive ("neutral") situations. A variety of intonation patterns, also, are introduced in the two drill books.

Analysis on Which These Materials Are Based

The lack of uniformity in analyzing stress and intonation

There is no unanimity among linguists as to the analytic treatment of stress, intonation, and juncture, though in the United States the analysis originally set forth by George L. Trager and Henry L. Smith, Jr., in their *Outline of English Structure* (1951), has wide currency. Many practicing linguists today accept the major features of it. It seems possible that the transformational-generative approach, at the present time concentrating more on syntax than on phonology, may eventually have an effect on the analysis and teaching of the prosodic features of language. At the moment, however, it is not easy to see just what this will be.

The Trager-Smith analysis is the one used here. It is practical and, by now, familiar. The English language teaching materials prepared by the American Council of Learned Societies in the early and mid-1950's were based on it. It is similar enough to the methods used in many other materials so that a teacher trained in other systems can use it. Slight modifications have been made here and there for pedagogical purposes. The symbols used for marking are our own; not all elements of the classical Trager-Smith analysis are used; and regular English orthography is used throughout (with minor exceptions).

The fact that analysts disagree, of course, does not change the living language in any way. Thus, the drill materials presented in these books, since they are based on real English, will no doubt be useful to any teacher, regardless of the particular system or analysis he may be most familiar with or may favor.

Analytical framework of these materials

The following brief discussion outlines the analytical framework within which the drill materials have been constructed and presented.

A sentence is understood to be an utterance bounded by silence at either end which is spoken as, and felt to be, a complete unit by a speaker. (He was not interrupted in the middle, nor did he stop before he had finished.) Every sentence has at least one phrase, but may have more than one.

Pitch and intonation. There are four pitch levels, mutually contrasting phonemically, called respectively, beginning with the lowest, pitch 1, pitch 2, pitch 3, and pitch 4. Pitch levels are relative, not absolute. An intonation pattern is a sequence of one or more pitches together with a phrase-ending contour. Intonation patterns are represented graphically by a heavy dark line superimposed on four horizontal lines printed above a text in regular orthographic symbols, much like a musical staff with words underneath.

Every phrase ends in one of three types of contour:

(1) *A rise in pitch.* The rise occurs on the last syllable, and reaches a point below the next higher pitch. The rise is represented in the drill material by a rising arrow:

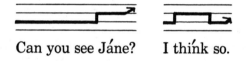

Can you see Jáne?   I thínk so.

(2) *A fading away into silence*, not accompanied by a terminal rise. There is often a fall in pitch, especially if the phrase ends on pitch 1. The fading away is represented by a break or space between the four horizontal lines, and the absence of an upturned arrow.

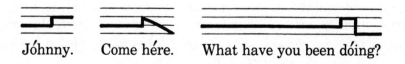

Jóhnny.   Come hére.   What have you been dóing?

(3) *A slowing down*, or sustension of the voice, not accompanied by a pitch rise or a fading away. This kind of phrase-ending contour has been described as a "shifting of gears." A dotted vertical line is used to represent this contour.

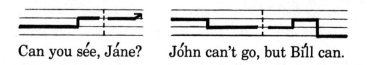

Can you sée, Jáne?   Jóhn can't go, but Bíll can.

One other convention is used in the drill materials. It does not represent a fourth terminal contour, but rather contour (1) above when it is not final in the sentence or utterance. The rising arrow and the dotted vertical line are both used in such cases, as in the following examples:

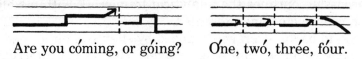

As used in the two drillbooks, the term 'phrase' may be defined as an utterance bounded by two terminal contours (or junctures), or beginning from silence and ending with one of them.

Needless to say, the intonation lines are only a schematic representation of what actually happens in natural speech. A level line does not represent pitch that is absolutely, monotonously, level. Generally, within any one pitch level, there are rises and falls in the pitch, associated with stress. Syllables with secondary stress, for instance, will quite often be spoken with slightly higher pitch than adjacent syllables with minor stress (or sometimes lower—either departure from "normal" causes the syllables to become prominent to that extent). Thus, there are small ups and downs within any one pitch level even though it is marked by a continuous straight line.

Stress and juncture. Four levels of stress are recognized. Stress is defined as the relative intensity or loudness with which a syllable is spoken. The four levels, beginning with the loudest, are designated as follows:

	Trager-Smith	This book	Examples
primary	xx́x	xx̄x	ít; sée; belíeve
secondary	xx̂x	xxx	strong mén; birds sing
tertiary	xx̀x	xxx	áshtray; unnécessary
weak	xx̌x*	xxx	imáginable; vénomously

The major-minor stress distinction. The distinction between major stress (primary or secondary) and minor stress (tertiary or weak) is extremely useful in English, and an understanding of it will clarify many points in the stressing of words in phrases. Major stress occurs on items that are members of the four syntactic word classes in English: noun, verb, adjective, and adverb, unless an item that ordinarily belongs to one of these classes has entered into a syntactic combination that requires its stress to be reduced to minor (usually tertiary). For example, the noun *tray* would normally be major-stressed, as in *Give me the tráy* or *This tray is too héavy*. However, when it becomes part of the noun compound *áshtray*, its stress is obligatorily reduced to tertiary; this reduction, in fact, is one of the main signals in English that such compounding has occurred. It is found in such items as *táke-off, léan-to, hótplate, stróng man* (a professional gymnast, not just a man who is strong), etc. Minor stress, on the other hand, occurs naturally on such items as personal pronouns, short prepositions, auxiliary verbs (unless in combination with *-n't*), etc., except when these items have special shifted or contrastive stress, as in *I said hím, not hér*. Failure to speak minor-stressed items with the proper reduced stress causes one's English to sound wrong to native speakers and it can even interfere with intelligibility. Many minor-stressed items vary freely between weak and tertiary stress, according to rhythmic considerations. For example, the kind of alternation that is heard in *sóme óf it* as opposed to *sóme of it*, or

* or unmarked.

give it to her as opposed to *give it to (h)er,** is meaningless and unpredictable, and if this were the whole story, there would be no phonemic distinction between weak and tertiary stress. However, there are other cases in which the difference between tertiary and weak is not a matter of choice and is therefore phonemic: e.g., the stress on the last syllables of *milkman* and *gentleman*, or *refugee* and *effigy*.

Primary (ʹ) is the strongest stress in a phrase. Every word spoken in isolation has primary stress on one syllable, the other syllables having one of the weaker stresses. Two successive primaries do not occur without one of the phrase-ending contours, already described, between them. A primary stress and a secondary stress do not occur without at least open juncture (roughly, a word-boundary, usually symbolized by space in writing) between them.

Secondary stress (—), a kind of reduced primary, is not recognized by all analysts. It occurs only on major-stressed items that have entered into syntactic combinations. It differentiates, in a well-known example from Trager and Smith's *Outline of English Structure*, *the white house* (not the yellow one) from *the White House* (the presidential mansion in Washington). Failure to master secondary stress, and to distinguish it from tertiary, can cause a speaker's English to sound quite unnatural and may even interfere with communication, as when *can*, normally tertiary or weak in verb phrases, is spoken with secondary stress and is mistaken for *can't* (American pronunciation), which normally has secondary.

Tertiary stress (-) is the "intermediate" stress recognized by all analysts of English in single words like *football*, *letdown* (noun), *undo*, *understand*, etc., and by many analysts in two-word phrases like *fountain pen*, *garden party*, etc. Its use in syntactic phrases has not been so widely recognized, but, as has been mentioned already, a great many syntactic relationships are signaled in English by giving minor stress, i.e., tertiary in most cases, to items that in independent use would have primary or secondary. Personal pronouns (*he, she, him, I, we, us*, etc.), short prepositions (*to, in, at, with*, etc.), auxiliary verbs (*is, have, will, must*, etc.) unless negated with -*n't*, and even lexical verbs in two-word verbs (*come in, take off, get on*, etc.) are normally spoken with minor stress and should have no more than tertiary stress. Failure to master tertiary stress in phrases leaves the student unprepared to use or understand many of the most important phonological signals in English.

Weak stress (·) is the level of least intensity. Most syllables spoken with weak stress are limited to certain vowels only, /ə/ and /ɨ/ being the favorites; others, according to dialect, are /iy/, /uw/, /i/, and sometimes /ey/ (as in *Sunday*) and /ow/ (as in *window*). Most speakers never say the vowels /æ/, /a/, /ɔ/, /u/, or /e/, or the glides /ay/ and /aw/ with weak stress; that is, any syllable containing these sounds automatically has at least tertiary stress. Speakers of languages without such elaborate stress systems as English have difficulty making the weak syllables weak enough, and their English as a result sounds exaggeratedly precise, over-formal, or just peculiar and difficult to understand. When a string of minor-stressed words occur together, tertiary and weak stresses can alternate, more or less unpredictably; in other cases, the difference between tertiary and weak stress is not a matter of choice, as has already been pointed out.

---

* Most English speakers regularly drop /h/ in a syllable that does not have at least tertiary stress. Contrary to the objections of purists, this is perfectly regular and correct. Thus, a speaker may say *to him* or *to 'im*; only the most careful speakers ever say *to him*.

A note on open juncture. This phenomenon is not specifically drilled in *Stress and Intonation, Parts 1 and 2*, but some examples of it are given in *Consonants and Vowels*. It is part of the English prosodic system and needs to be mentioned. If spoken English models are provided, the student will automatically get practice in using it. So-called open juncture, sometimes called "plus-juncture" (from the habit of some linguists of indicating it in their transcriptions by a plus sign) or even just "juncture," is the phonological signal that separates items like *an aim* and *a name*, or *night rate* and *nitrate*, to use two examples that have become classic. The phonetic nature of the feature is quite complex, but the point is that all English speakers are aware that there is something that "keeps words apart" in English utterances. A great many other languages in the world have no such feature at all. It has been said that in ordinary fast speech, the syllables follow each other in French and Spanish with no regard for word boundaries at all.

SPECIAL NOTES

Regular Orthography Used

Regular English orthography is used in the two drill books, except for a few instances (Section 11, Part 1). A key to the symbols used is given on page xix, Part 1. Although the use of regular orthography presents some minor difficulty in marking stresses over vowel nuclei, as well as with syllabification, there are obvious advantages in not introducing a transcription system. Regular dictionary rules are followed in syllabifying words, even when such division does not exactly match the phonetic facts.

Stresses Correlated with Grammatical Patterns

Correlating stresses with grammatical patterns sometimes results in over-simplification. It may even seem to stretch the language here and there. However, this technique provides at least a starting point for the student in hearing and practicing basic stress and rhythm patterns of the language. Once the student has had practice with the kind of material in these drill books and has worked with the major-minor stress distinction, the teacher should then find it easier to use unmarked text material with him.

Some Variation in Stress Permissible

Almost anything in English can be correctly intoned and stressed in more than one way, especially when several dialects are involved. What has been done in these books is to select one possibility—hopefully, the most frequent or most likely one—and give extensive drill on it For example, noun compounds are presented as having primary-tertiary stress (*bláckbȳrd, bláckbōard*, etc.). It is understood that the second element of the compound may have secondary stress in the speech of many persons (bláckbōard), or that the stress of the second element may vary unpredictably between tertiary and secondary (bláckbīrd, bláckboārd), and that the second element is especially likely to have secondary stress if either element in the compound has more than one syllable (végetáblé gārdén). These matters are not very important in the context of these drill books. The important thing for the student is that the major stress must occur on the first element and that such items as gréenhōuse and grēen hóuse must be distinguished. If he makes the last two syllables in the following sentences homophonous, it doesn't matter; there are many English speakers who do the same:

Īt's nōt à whité hōuse; īt's à gréen hōuse.

Wé grōw flowérs īn thé gréenhōuse.

However, if the student stresses (and uses high pitch on) the last syllable of the following sentence, he has made a mistake:

Wrong: Kēep thé flowérs īn thé greenhóuse.

It is extremely difficult to distinguish with certainty between two adjacent stresses in certain environments. One is often hard put to it to decide whether a stress is weak or tertiary, tertiary or secondary, or even secondary or primary. In many cases, fortunately, it is not crucial to decide. Although certain stresses are indicated in the textbooks as occurring with certain grammatical categories, the student is not asked to distinguish between them in the exercises. Nor is any particular advantage seen in having students mark sentences or passages for stress and intonation. The important and most useful thing is to drill items that are problems for learners, such as the location of the high pitch and primary stress in sentences like these:

Ī càn dó ìt.

Shē's tāllér thàn I ́am.

Hē wàs hónést àbout ìt.

In addition, students should be corrected at all times when they make mistakes in either stress or intonation.

Pre-recorded Tapes

Pre-recorded tapes accompany each of the drill books. Each tape is twenty to thirty minutes in length. These tapes are recorded on 5 inch reels at $3\frac{3}{4}$ ips. In the main, items are given for listening practice and for repetition practice. The tapes must not be considered a substitute for the teacher, since only the teacher can isolate problems, make explanations when needed, make corrections, and conduct drill. The tapes can help the teacher by providing endless drill, repeating the material tirelessly and without change. Part of the student's problem, too, is learning to hear differences. After having careful attention called to certain matters, he then needs to listen. The tapes can be extremely helpful in this respect.

Word List

At the end of Section 11 is a word list, giving numerous examples of words with various stress patterns. It is difficult to find such lists of words, and this one is presented for the convenience of teachers who may want to construct their own drills on certain patterns or who may need additional examples to use in class. The suggested words can be used as a start and then filled in with examples of the teacher's own choosing if he wishes.

How These Materials Can Be Used

In basic or elementary level courses, it is admittedly difficult to make use of materials of the kind presented here, for lack of time and because much of the vocabulary in these materials is beyond elementary levels. However, even in the early stages of language learning, these materials can be used selectively in order to supply drill material on specific points. Later on, in intermediate and advanced classes, the materials can be worked into the program with ease, either as a regular part of the course or as special supplementary drill on pronunciation problems. The materials can be used consecutively or selectively, according to the teacher's preference. They will easily find a place in teachers' seminars or in brush-up courses, where supplementary material is always needed. Finally, there are always the highly motivated and especially skilled students in any group who are able to spend more time and effort on their study, and who will, no doubt, find these books helpful in gaining mastery of the stress and intonational systems of English.

KEY TO SYMBOLS USED

Vowel Sounds

/æ/	cat, had	/ay/	bite, buy
/e/	bet, said	/ey/	bait, came
/i/	bit, miss	/iy/	beet, team
/a/	pot, rob	/oy/	boy, coin
/ə/	but, come nátion, upón	/aw/ /ow/	cow, how no, blow
/ɔ/	bought, saw	/uw/	bloom, shoe
/u/	put, foot		

Consonant Sounds

/p/	pen, úpper	/s/	see, class
/t/	ten, bútter	/z/	zone, his
/k/	kick, come	/š/	shoe, cash
/b/	bad, rúbber	/ž/	leisure, tréasure
/d/	den, sádder	/č/	check, catch
/g/	get, forgót	/j/	jug, barge
/f/	fine, cóffee	/θ/	thin, bath
/v/	vine, héavy	/ð/	then, bathe
/m/	man, come	/y/	yéllow, yes
/n/	no, on	/w/	walk, win
/ŋ/	sing, sínging	/h/	him, home
/l/	long, píllow		
/r/	rod, bar		

1. INTRODUCTION

(Tape 1 begins here)

This book will give you practice drill with two aspects of English speech — stress and intonation. Learning to manipulate these two features will improve both your speech and your comprehension of spoken English.

The English Writing System

Written English consists mainly of letters which represent the consonant and vowel sounds of spoken English. As you know, the writing system is not very consistent in the way it represents the speech sounds of English. Written English gives very little help with either stress or intonation. There are a few punctuation marks which give clues to stress and intonation, such as the period (.) (you stop speaking); the comma (,) (usually a slight hesitation); the question mark (?) (a question with a rising or falling voice); and the exclamation point (!) (a word in the sentence is emphasized), and two or three others. Aside from these few punctuation marks, which in themselves are not always reliable guides, there is nothing else in the writing system that shows how to say something with the proper stress and intonation.

In this book we shall use some marks and lines to represent both stress and intonation, and give you ample opportunity to drill and practice the features of both systems.

Intonation

Intonation is the rise and fall of the voice. Intonation can make a difference in meaning. For example, if you say *He's coming* with a falling voice at the end, you are making a statement. If you say it with a rising voice, you are asking a question.

Statement *Question*

He's coming. He's coming?

1

There are four levels which we use when speaking. We shall represent these levels by four horizontal lines. Each line will represent a level. The lowest is pitch level 1. The highest is pitch level 4.

```
4 _____
3 _____
2 _____
1 _____
```

Declarative Intonation

In an affirmative or negative statement, most sentences begin on level 2, rise to level 3, and then go down to pitch 1. If we say a sentence such as *John is my brother*, we can show the rise and fall of the voice by musical notes.

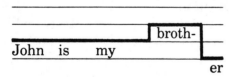

Here are a few more sentences which we would say in the same way.

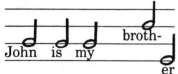

He is my father.
Helen's my sister.
They are his parents.
I need a haircut.

Instead of musical notes, we shall in this book use a heavy dark line to indicate intonation.

Here are some more sentences which would be said in the same way.

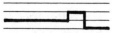

He is my father.
Helen's my sister.
She is my mother.
They are my parents.

Many times the voice does not step down as is shown above. It often glides down. For example, if the last word has only one syllable, it would look like this:

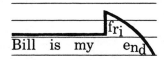

Bill is my friend.

Here are a few more examples:

Bill is my friend.
John is a boy.
Mary's a girl.
This is my book.
I have a car.

Practice Sentences

Practice saying these sentences. Begin on pitch level 2. Go to pitch 3 on the syllable that is italicized, and then go down to pitch level 1.

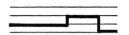

I have a *broth*er.
She has a *sist*er.
I need some *pap*er.
He has a *pen*cil.
We want to *study*.

Now practice these sentences which glide down rather than step down.

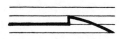

He is my *friend.*
She is a *nurse.*
This is a *pen.*
That is a *book.*
I have a *car.*

Sentences which begin with question words are said in the same way. The question words include: *who, what, when, where, why, which, how long, how far*, etc.

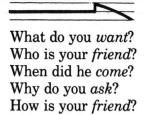

What do you *want*?
Who is your *friend*?
When did he *come*?
Why do you *ask*?
How is your *friend*?

If the last word has more than one syllable, then your voice steps down.

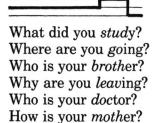

What did you *study*?
Where are you *going*?
Who is your *brother*?
Why are you *leaving*?
Who is your *doctor*?
How is your *mother*?

Question Intonation

Another common intonation is one in which the voice rises at the end. In this kind of question, we begin on pitch level 2. The voice goes to pitch 3 and then continues to glide a little higher.

If we use musical notes, the sentences below would look like this:

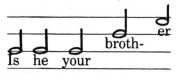

Is he your *brother*?
Is she your *sister*?
Are they his *parents*?
Do you need *paper*?
Have you seen *Helen*?

We shall use a line, again, to indicate the levels of the voice. To show the little rise at the end of the question, we shall use a small arrow pointing upwards to indicate that the voice goes a little higher than the pitch 3 level.

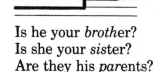

Is he your *brother*?
Is she your *sister*?
Are they his *parents*?
Do you need *paper*?
Have you seen *Helen*?

We shall use the same kind of line with an arrow when the word ends in one syllable.

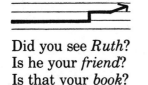

Did you see *Ruth*?
Is he your *friend*?
Is that your *book*?
Have you seen *Jim*?

Now practice these questions and answers

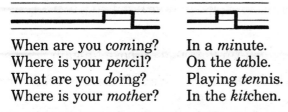

Can you *go*?	Yes, I *can*.
Does she *sing*?	Yes, she *does*.
May I *help*?	Yes, you *may*.
Did he *come*?	Yes, he *did*.
Can you *hear*?	Yes, I *can*.

Listen to these questions and answers, and then practice them.

When are you *coming*?	In a *minute*.
Where is your *pencil*?	On the *table*.
What are you *doing*?	Playing *tennis*.
Where is your *mother*?	In the *kitchen*.

It is important to know that the pitch levels do not represent the same absolute level for all speakers. Everyone has his own range. A man with a low voice speaks on the four levels in his key. A woman with a high voice speaks on the four levels in her range.

Another thing to remember is that the lines we have put on paper to represent intonation, and the lines which you will use as a guide to the ups and downs of the voice while speaking, give only a general idea of what happens when people speak. Your best progress will come when you listen as closely as you can to people who speak the language, and endeavor to imitate them as closely as you can. The lines and markings in this book should help give you some idea of what happens when people speak, but there is no substitute for listening, practicing, and imitating.

Stress

Stress is the degree of loudness or force with which syllables are spoken in English. Every word in English is made up of one or more syllables. Here are a few examples.

one syllable	*two syllables*	*three syllables*
go	go-ing	re-mem-ber
come	com-ing	con-tin-ue
book	pa-per	cal-en-dar
see	vis-it	vis-it-ing

If you wish to know how many syllables a word has, the best place to look is in the dictionary. All dictionaries divide words into syllables.

When a word has two syllables, one syllable is always said louder than the other. Here are some examples.

going	*go*-ing	*go* is louder than *ing*
study	*stud*-y	*stud* is louder than *y*
pencil	*pen*-cil	*pen* is louder than *cil*
paper	*pa*-per	*pa* is louder than *per*
ago	a-*go*	*go* is louder than *a*
above	a-*bove*	*bove* is louder than *a*
again	a-*gain*	*gain* is louder than *a*

If a word has three syllables, one syllable is always louder than the other two.

remember	re-*mem*-ber	*mem* is louder than *re* and *ber*
continue	con-*tin*-ue	*tin* is louder than *con* and *ue*
agreement	a-*gree*-ment	*gree* is louder than *a* and *ment*
calendar	*cal*-en-dar	*cal* is louder than *en* and *dar*

The loudest or strongest stress is called primary stress. We shall use a little mark over the syllable with the loudest stress to indicate that this is the syllable with primary stress.

gó-ing   stúd-y   re-mém-ber   con-tín-ue   a-gó   a-bóve   a-gáin

The softest or weakest stress is called weak stress. We will use a small dot over the syllables that have weak stress.

gó-ing   stúd-ẏ   rė-mém-bėr   cȯn-tín-uė   ȧ-gó   ȧ-bóve   ȧ-gáin

In English every word has one primary stress when it is spoken in isolation; that is, if only the one word is spoken. You can find the primary stress of a word by looking in any English dictionary. When two or more words are spoken in a phrase, however, only one of the words retains its primary stress. The primary stresses of the other word or words in the phrase are reduced. In this book we shall mark four different degrees of loudness. The two loudest stresses we shall call primary stress and secondary stress. These are major stresses. The two weaker stresses are called tertiary stress and weak stress. These are minor stresses. We shall use marks above the syllables to indicate different stresses, as follows:

Type	*Name of Stress*	*Symbol*	*Example*
Major Stress	{Primary Stress	′	Īt's ȧ blāck bóok.
	{Secondary Stress	—	Īt's ȧ black bóok.
Minor Stress	{Tertiary Stress	⁻	Īt's ȧ blāck bóok.
	{Weak Stress	•	Īt's ȧ blāck bóok.

Stress and Intonation

Everything that is spoken in English, a word, phrase, or sentence, is spoken with both stress and intonation.

We shall not always mark the intonation in this book. If a word or sentence is not marked, you should use the declarative intonation when reading or practicing. In the declarative intonation your voice begins on the pitch 2 level. Everything is said on the 2 level until you reach the primary stress. On the syllable with primary stress your voice rises to the 3 level. Following this syllable, your voice either steps down or glides down to pitch level 1 where the remainder of the word or sentence is spoken. Here are a few examples of the declarative intonation.

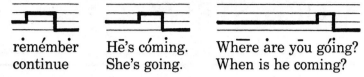

remémber   He's cóming.   Whēre ạre yōu góing?
continue   She's going.   When is he coming?

Sometimes the primary stress of a word comes on the first syllable. In this case, your voice begins on the 3 level and then steps down to the 1 level. This is also the declarative intonation. Some words, of course, have only one syllable. In speaking words of this kind, your voice begins on level 3 and glides down to level 1. This also is the declarative intonation. Here are some examples of words of both kinds.

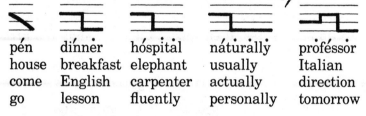

pén   dínnẹr   hóspitạl   nátụrạllỵ   proféssọr
house   breakfast elephant   usually   Italian
come   English   carpenter   actually   direction
go   lesson   fluently   personally   tomorrow

You are now ready to begin section two.

2. WORD STRESS (1)

Words with Primary and Weak Stress *(Tape 2 begins here)*

First listen to the words and sentences; then repeat them. Change the article *a* to *an* wherever necessary in the drills.

1. ′	2. ′ •	3. ′ • •	4. ′ • • •
pen	dinner	hospital	naturally
house	breakfast	elephant	usually
come	English	carpenter	actually
go	lesson	fluently	personally
black	hundred	studying	temperature
green	study	visited	perishable
two	visit	excellent	manageable
soon	yellow	seventy	miserable

Drill A

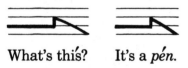

What's this?   It's a *pén.*

′	′ •	′ • •
pen	pencil	calendar
book	table	radio
desk	picture	bicycle

Drill B

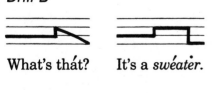

What's thát?   It's a *swéater.*

′	′ •	′ • •
cat	package	elephant
coat	garden	animal
bus	sweater	formula

Drill C

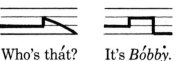

Who's thát?   It's *Bóbby̆*.

′	′ •	′ • •
John	Mary	Harriet
Bill	Bobby	Barbara
June	Janice	Meredith

Drill D

That's Jóhn.   He's a *dóctŏr*.

′	′ •	′ • •
cook	doctor	jeweler
friend	dentist	messenger
guest	sailor	specialist

5. ′   6. • ′   7. • ′ •   8. • ′ •   9. • ′ • •

5.	6.	7.	8.	9.
car	hello	professor	community	immediately
boy	asleep	Italian	material	occasionally
do	Japan	direction	experience	approximately
know	ago	tomorrow	developmenι	considerably
Spain	result	important	emergency	cooperative
one	today	eleven	ability	mysteriously
here	above	preparing	Bolivia	exceptionally

Drill E

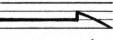

Where's he fróm?   He's from *Japán*.

′	• ′	• ′ •	• ′ • •
France	Peru	Alaska	Bolivia
Greece	Japan	Malaya	Colombia
Spain	Tibet	Nebraska	Bavaria

Drill F

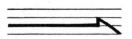 

What does he dó?   He's a *proféssŏr*.

• ′ •	• ′ • •
policeman	photographer
reporter	stenographer
musician	philosopher
mechanic	astronomer

Drill G

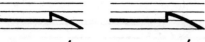

What's thát?   It's a *machíne*.

boat	machine	tomato
car	parade	banana
bus	sedan	diploma
bank	alarm	piano
spoon	guitar	eraser
key	surprise	potato
check	report	recorder

Drill H

Is that his *pícture*?

pen	pencil	machine	elephant	decision	experiment
book	table	guitar	animal	banana	discovery
coat	picture	surprise	formula	eraser	thermometer

Drill I

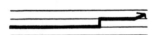

Are you from *África*?

France	Ghana	Brazil	Africa	Alaska	Bolivia
Spain	Guinea	Japan	Italy	Nebraska	Colombia
Greece	China	Peru	Sicily	Australia	Bavaria

Drill J

He's *Gérman*.

French	Spanish	Indian	Malayan	Bolivian
Greek	English	Libyan	Italian	Colombian
Thai	German	Mexican	Egyptian	Peruvian
Dutch	Russian	Chilean	Moroccan	American

There are a few pairs of words in English which are pronounced almost the same except for their stress. Below are a few words of this kind. Those in the left column are verbs. Those in the right column are nouns.

• /	/ •
record	record
present	present
rebel	rebel
desert	desert

Exercise 1

Below is a list of words. Listen to them and decide in which column they belong according to the kind of stress they have.

	/ •	• /	• / •
1. angry	angry		
2. above		above	
3. professor			professor
4. belief			
5. decided			
6. wanted			
7. movie			
8. hotel			
9. enjoy			
10. example			
11. remembered			
12. people			
13. forget			
14. because			
15. roses			

Exercise 2

One of the words below does not have the same stress as the others. Can you tell which one it is?

example   gentleman
conductor   preparing
Kentucky

The one that is different is _____.

Exercise 3

Do all of the words below have the same stress?

háppy	twenty
corner	sixty
many	coming
seven	going

(Yes or no) _____

Exercise 4

Below are pairs of words. Listen carefully and decide whether they have the same stress pattern or whether the stress patterns are different.

	Same	Different
1. refer reefer		X
2. table pencil	X	
3. professor architect		
4. accept accent		
5. comforting exciting		
6. amusing important		
7. winter weather		

Exercise 5

Listen to these words. Put a circle around the syllable which has the primary stress.

1.	money	(mon)-ey
2.	perhaps	per-(haps)
3.	selection	se-(lec)-tion
4.	temperature	tem-per-a-ture
5.	after	af-ter
6.	permit	per-mit
7.	employment	em-ploy-ment
8.	marvelous	mar-vel-ous
9.	modern	mod-ern
10.	perishable	per-ish-a-ble
11.	continue	con-tin-ue
12.	industrial	in-dus-trial
13.	happily	hap-pi-ly
14.	because	be-cause
15.	fortunately	for-tu-nate-ly
16.	nothing	noth-ing
17.	amusing	a-mus-ing
18.	possibly	pos-si-bly
19.	deter	de-ter
20.	conclusion	con-clu-sion

Words with Tertiary Stress   *(Tape 3 begins here)*

The words in this section have tertiary stress as well as primary and weak. Tertiary stress is spoken a little louder or with a little more force than weak stress. We shall use a very short line above the syllable to indicate tertiary stress.

Listen to the words below and imitate them as closely as you can, paying particular attention to the stress patterns.

1. ′ ⁻	2. ′ • ⁻	3. ′ • ⁻ •
athlete	exercise	dictionary
contract	telephone	elevator
program	envelope	necessary
translate	Portuguese	February
also	institute	secretary
income	emphasize	agriculture
elbow	holiday	territory
import	realize	emphasizes
export	telescope	exercises
Denmark	boulevard	fascinating

Drill A

What's thát?   It's my *prógrăm.*

′ ⁻	′ • ⁻	′ • ⁻ •
program	telephone	dictionary
costume	envelope	television
elbow	magazine	dormitory

Drill B

Who's thát?   That's *Bárbără.*

′ • •	′ • ⁻
Angela	Annabelle
Barbara	Genevieve
Catherine	Hildegarde
Beatrice	Josephine

Drill C

′ • ⁻	′ • ⁻ •
telephone	telephoning
emphasize	emphasizing
operate	operating
supervise	supervising
occupy	occupying
simplify	simplifying
classify	classifying

Drill D

Below are some pairs of related words. Notice the different stress patterns. Note also that there is a difference in the last vowel of each pair.

′ • •	′ • –
separate (*adj.*)	separate (*v.*)
duplicate (*n.*)	duplicate (*v.*)
intimate (*adj.*)	intimate (*v.*)
emphasis (*n.*)	emphasize (*v.*)

4. ‾ ′
almost
Chinese
engrave
routine
northeast
southwest
fourteen
eighteen
fifteen

5. ‾ • ′
understand
engineer
Japanese
guarantee
souvenir
lemonade
employee
Congolese
seventeen

6. ‾ • ′ •
information
education
occupation
engineering
Argentina
invitation
mathematics
population
transportation

7. ‾ • ′ • •
nationality
secretarial
cafeteria
university
satisfactory
hippopotamus
anniversary
Ecuadorian
Ethiopian

Drill E

What's his nātionálity?   He's *Jāpánése.*

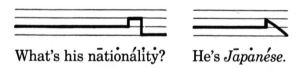

‾ • ′	‾ • ′ •	‾ • ′ ••
Japanese	Guatemalan	Ecuadorian
Congolese	Uruguayan	Ethiopian
Lebanese	Paraguayan	Argentinean

Drill F

Is he an *ácròbāt?*

′ • –	‾ • ′
diplomat	engineer
acrobat	employee
democrat	pioneer

Drill G

′ ·	− ′
thirty	thirteen
forty	fourteen
fifty	fifteen
sixty	sixteen
eighty	eighteen
ninety	nineteen

There are many different word stress patterns which include a tertiary stress. Below are examples of some of the patterns in which the primary stress comes at or near the beginning of the word.

8. ′ − ·
translator
located
library

9. ′ · · −
automobile
characterize
alienate

10. ′ ·· − ·
patriotism
characterizes
capitalizes

11. · ′ · −
appreciate
aristocrat
dissatisfy

12. · ′ · · ·
appreciated
refrigerator
imaginary

The patterns below all have a tertiary stress which comes before the primary stress.

13. − ′ ·
idea
translation
northeastern

14. −′ · ·
geography
spectacular
transparency

15. · − · ′ ·
examination
pronunciation
communication

16. · − · ′ ··
encyclopedia
attainability

17. ·− · ′ ·
cooperation
negotiation

18. · − ·· ′ ·
materialistic

19. − · ′ · · ·
unintelligible
conversationalist

20. − · · ′ ·
recommendation
mathematician

21. − · ′ · ·
educationist
inspirational

22. · − · ′·· ·
impossibility

Exercise 1

Below are words of three syllables. Can you tell where the primary stress is?

	first syllable	second syllable	third syllable
1. understand			understánd
2. northeastern		northeástern	
3. telephone	télephone		
4. library			
5. seventeen			
6. infection			
7. hemisphere			
8. emphasis			
9. multiply			
10. idea			
11. introduce			
12. realize			
13. disbelieve			
14. televise			
15. unfeeling			

Exercise 2

Below are five words. One of them has a different stress pattern from the others. Can you find it?

1. designate   3 Portuguese   5. terrified
2. emphasize   4. disregard   The word that is different is _____

Exercise 3

Put a circle around the syllable which has the primary stress.

1. convenient   con-(ven)-ient   9. sixteen   six-teen
2. appreciated   ap-(pre)-ci-at-ed   10. imagination   im-ag-i-na-tion
3. orchestra   or-ches-tra   11. stimulating   stim-u-lat-ing
4. pronunciation   pro-nun-ci-a-tion   12. revolutionized rev-o-lu-tion-ized
5. industrious   in-dus-tri-ous   13. remarkably   re-mark-a-bly
6. principal   prin-ci-pal   14. sixty   six-ty
7. recreation   rec-re-a-tion   15. perfectly   per-fect-ly
8. opportunity   op-por-tu-ni-ty

Exercise 4

Each of the pairs of words below has the same number of syllables. Is the primary stress of each pair on the same or on a different syllable?

	Same	Different
1. machine picture		X
2. telephone understand		X
3. dictionary television	X	
4. above early		
5. diplomat engineer		
6. forty fourteen		
7. coming working		
8. telephone operate		
9. emphasizes exercises		
10. ago above		
11. arriving department		
12. understand diplomat		
13. calendar remember		
14. Africa Alaska		
15. result machine		
16. obey study		
17. information necessary		

	Same	Different
18. weather summer		
19. mistake error		
20. material experience		
21. telephone televise		
22. animal direction		
23. experience information		
24. electrician electrical		
25. mechanical mechanizes		

Exercise 5

Pronounce the words below with the proper stress. All of these words are from the drill material.

1. today	7. photographer	13. usually	19. translate
2. experience	8. experiment	14. appreciated	20. university
3. machine	9. direction	15. telephone	21. northeast
4. Africa	10. result	16. telephoning	22. emphasize
5. above	11. hundred	17. engineer	23. geography
6. mechanic	12. studying	18. population	24. impossibility
			25. cooperation

3. WORD STRESS (2)
NOUN COMPOUNDS

This section will give you practice with noun compounds. In order to speak English correctly, it is essential that you understand noun compounds and use the proper stress when speaking them.

Noun compounds are composed of two separate words. There are two important things to remember about them.

(1) Noun compounds function as a single noun.

(2) Noun compounds have a stress pattern of primary-tertiary.

The first word of the compound has a primary stress; the second word has a tertiary stress as its loudest stress.

Noun compounds are written in three different ways. Many are written as single words. Others are written as two words. A few are written with a hyphen between the two words.

Written as one word	*as two words*	*hyphenated*
classroom	fountain pen	bath-towel

There is no way to be sure how to write a noun compound. English dictionaries differ as to whether certain noun compounds should be written as one word, two words, or with a hyphen. Whichever form you find in the particular dictionary you are using will be acceptable.

Both parts of a noun compound may be nouns, or one part may be an adjective, a preposition or a verb. Regardless of how they are formed, you can recognize them by their stress pattern and by their function in a sentence. Here are some examples of noun compounds, each part of which is composed of only one syllable.

1. ′ ‾	2. ′ ‾	*(Tape 4 begins here)*
classroom	blackboard	
schoolboy	high school	
farmhouse	forehead	
teapot	rowboat	
railroad	washcloth	
suitcoat	headache	
wristwatch	highway	
armchair	chopsticks	
football	haircut	
housewife	shipwreck	

Drill A

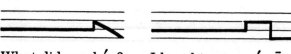

What did you búy?   I bought some *pópcōrn*.

ice skates
popcorn
school books
washcloths
light bulbs
golf clubs

Drill B

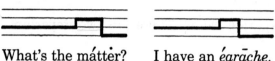

What's the mátter?   I have an *éarăche*.

toothache
earache
backache
headache
head cold
chest cold

Drill C

Does he go to schóol?   Yés.   He goes to *hígh schōol*.

high school
grade school
night school
day school

Drill D

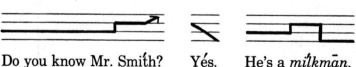

Do you know Mr. Smíth?   Yés.   He's a *mílkmān*.

bank clerk
mailman
milkman
file clerk

Drill E

For breakfast we had *frúit jūice*.

´ -
cornflakes
bran flakes
fruit juice
grape juice
pancakes

When either or both parts of a noun compound have more than one syllable, the noun compound still has the same basic stress pattern of primary-tertiary. That is, the first word of the compound has primary stress on one of the syllables; the loudest stress of the second word is tertiary stress.

3. ´ · -

apple tree
weatherman
grammar book
grocery store
fountain pen
water glass
pocketknife
dining room
tennis ball
summertime

4. ´ - ·

newspaper
typewriter
post office
bus driver
schoolteacher
grandfather
ink bottle
fire engine
wastebasket
gas station

Drill F

I bought some

´ - ·
pineapples.
tea biscuits.
beef liver.

I got them at the
I got them at the
I got it at the

´ · -
grocery store.
pastry shop.
butcher's shop.

Drill G

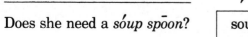

Does she need a *sóup spōon*?

´ -	´ · -	´ - ·
soup spoon	sugar bowl	cream pitcher
soup bowl	salad fork	meat platter
steak knife	water glass	salt shaker
wineglass	tablecloth	breadbasket
teapot	dinner plate	soup ladle
teaspoon	butter knife	cake server

Drill H

Are you going to wear a *súit cōat?*

> suit coat
> topcoat
> raincoat
> rain hat
> dress shirt
> sport shirt

5.
flower garden
writing paper
office worker
filling station
tennis racquet
dancing partner
mountain climber
record changer
science teacher
swimming practice

6.
movie theater
toilet articles
letter carrier
office manager
traffic accident
travel agency
army officer
lumber company
dental specialist
music festival

7.
department store
tobacco shop
election year
piano store
appointment book
banana stem
vanilla bean
discussion group
amusement park
assembly plant

8.
fire department
tax collector
news reporter
train conductor
car mechanic
mail delivery
steel production
speech improvement
fire prevention
farm equipment

Drill I

Have you seen Bób?   Yes.   He's in the *bárber shōp.*

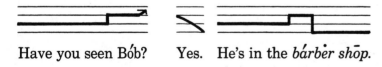

bookstore	barbershop	electric shop
drugstore	swimming pool	department store
lunchroom	coffee shop	amusement park
toy store	candy store	tobacco shop
shoe store	hobby shop	appliance store

Drill J

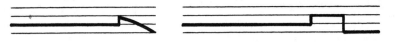

I'm going to the stóre.   I have to buy some *tóothpāste.*

, –	, • –	, – •
toothpaste	shaving cream	hair tonic
hand cream	razor blades	hand lotion
mouthwash	shower soap	bath powder

Drill K

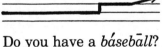

That's Mr. Whíte.   He's a *wéathèrmān.*

, –	, – •	,• – •
bank clerk	shoemaker	science teacher
mailman	watchmaker	factory worker
milkman	dressmaker	language teacher
fire chief	cabdriver	English teacher

Drill L

Do you have a *báseb̄all?*

, –	, • –
baseball	swimming suit
football	bowling ball
golf bag	punching bag
racehorse	fishing rod
rowboat	bathing suit
handball	fencing mask

Drill M

Do you need some *gólf b̄alls?*

, –	, • –
golf clubs	swimming trunks
ice skates	tennis balls
golf balls	water skis
track shoes	roller skates
ski poles	bowling shoes
snowshoes	camping gear

Below are examples of noun compounds with more elaborate stress patterns. Note that the first word of the compound always has a primary stress.

9.
police department
police equipment
research department

10.
smoking tobacco
dental appointment
Spanish professor

11.
detective story
committee meeting
employment office

12.
orchestra conductor
hospital attendant
history professor

13.
air conditioning
fire extinguisher

14.
reception committee

15.
arithmetic lesson

16.
vocational school

17.
furniture company

18.
construction company

19.
theater tickets

20.
population growth

21.
television set

22.
geography teacher

23.
engineering office

24.
library book

Exercise 1

In the following list there are two that are not noun compounds. You can tell by the stress. Can you find them?

1. drugstore   4. toothpaste   7. high school   10. mailbox
2. horse race   5. blackbird   8. campfire
3. haircut   6. red shoes   9. wool suit

Exercise 2

These are noun compounds which have not been used in this lesson. See if you can say them correctly the first time.

1. mail truck   8. plane trip   15. movie star
2. shoelaces   9. travel agency   16. drinking fountain
3. milk bottle   10. passport   17. heating system
4. bookkeeper   11. storybook   18. sunrise
5. tiepin   12. beauty parlor   19. wrapping paper
6. doorbell   13. road map   20. earthquake
7. sweetheart   14. birthplace

Exercise 3

Below is a list of words. Some of them are noun compounds and some are not. Listen carefully to your teacher or to the tape and mark the primary stress of each one. Remember, in a noun compound, there is only one primary stress—on the first part.

1. enginéer
2. políce car
3. candy
4. barbershop
5. umbrella
6. Japan
7. classroom
8. water glass
9. animal
10. fire prevention
11. exercise
12. bus driver
13. Spanish
14. suitcoat
15. appreciate
16. sixty
17. tablecloth
18. machine
19. sixteen
20. news reporter
21. education
22. furniture company
23. employment
24. electricity
25. office manager

Exercise 4

The noun compounds below are all from the drill material of this lesson. Try to read each one correctly.

1. classroom
2. haircut
3. wristwatch
4. headache
5, high school
6. shoe store
7. mailman
8. writing paper
9. newspaper
10. English teacher
11. summertime
12. movie theater
13. car mechanic
14. toilet articles
15. barbershop
16. fire department
17. election year
18. department store
19. population growth
20. engineering office

Exercise 5

Fill the blanks with noun compounds made from the two italicized words.

Example: A *store* which sells *drugs* is a <u>drugstore</u>.

1. A *store* which sells *groceries* is a _____.
2. A *ball* used in *bowling* is a _____.
3. A *man* who delivers *mail* is a _____.
4. A *knife* used for *butter* is a _____.
5. A *coat* you wear in the *rain* is a _____.
6. A *store* which sells *candy* is a _____.
7. A *store* which sells *furniture* is a _____.
8. *Water* which is good for *drinking* is called _____.
9. *Paper* used for *wrapping* things is called _____.
10. *Equipment* used on a *farm* is _____.
11. A *stamp* used for *postage* is a _____.
12. A *theater* which shows *movies* is a _____.
13. A *box* in which you keep *bread* is called a _____.
14. A *pot* used for making *coffee* is a _____.
15. A *train* which carries *passengers* is a _____.
16. A *man* who makes *repairs* is called a _____.
17. A *car* which runs on *cables* is called a _____.

18. A *mechanic* who works in a *garage* is a _____.
19. *Juice* made from *tomatoes* is called _____.
20. A *garden* in which you grow *vegetables* is a _____.

There are thousands of noun compounds in English. Learn to listen for them. Try to remember them, or better still, write them down in a notebook and use them every chance you have.

You can improve both your comprehension and pronunciation if you learn to recognize noun compounds and speak them with the proper stress pattern.

4. WORD COMBINATION STRESS (1)
MINOR STRESS

In previous sections we studied word stress. In this and succeeding sections we will have practice with word combination stress.

When two or more words are used together in a phrase, only one of the words retains its primary stress. For example, here are some one-syllable words, each of which has primary stress when spoken as a single word.

mý

his

book

car

If we combine the words into phrases, we have:

my book

his car

In these phrases, *book* and *car* are said with a louder stress than the words *my* and *his*. The stress pattern of the word combination is tertiary-primary.

mȳ bóok

hīs cár

In the two sentences below, you will notice that the primary stress of the nouns *lésson* and *díctionārȳ* has become secondary stress.

The ̇lessȯn wȧs hárd.

The ̇dictionārȳ is ̄in thė library.̇

Notice also that the words *the, was, is* have weak stress, and the word *in* has tertiary stress.

In one phrase there can be only one primary stress. The primary stresses of all the other words in the phrase or sentence become weaker. Some word stresses are reduced to secondary stress (a major stress), and other word stresses become tertiary or weak (minor stresses). This is done in a fairly regular manner. In general terms, we can say that content words, such as nouns, verbs, adjectives, and adverbs have major stress. The function words, such as prepositions, auxiliaries, articles, pronouns, have minor stress (either tertiary or weak). Although the function words are few in number, they are extremely common in speech. One very important aspect of learning to speak English well is the mastery of the use of the minor stresses in English. You will probably not have much success in improving your speech by learning rules. The most success will come after practicing and imitating to the best of your ability. The drill material which follows will give you the opportunity for a great deal of organized practice.

This section of the book presents drill material on certain grammatical categories which are regularly reduced to a minor stress when in combination with other kinds of words.

Tertiary Stress   *(Tape 5 begins here)*

The primary stress of words in this section usually becomes tertiary stress.

Subject Pronouns and Contractions

1. ‾ ′
    I came
    she sings
    we swim
    you know
    I've taught
    she's gone

2. ‾ ′ ·
    I studied
    we waited
    you promised
    they're coming
    she's worried
    he's waiting

3. ‾   ′ · ·
    they're finishing
    I visited
    she's wondering
    we're visiting
    he's worrying
    they're traveling

4. ‾ · ′
    I forget
    we began
    they've arrived

5. ‾ · ′ ·
    they remember
    he's deciding
    he commanded

6. ‾ · ′ · ·
    we're continuing
    he's examining
    she's remembering

7. ‾ ‾ · ′
    they understand
    she overslept
    they're guaranteed

8. ‾ ′ ‾
    he translates
    they export
    he broadcasts

9. ‾ ′ · ‾
    we telephoned
    she realized
    they've operated

10. ‾ ′ · · ·
    she realizes
    they're telephoning

11. · · ′ · ‾
    he appreciates
    they participate

12. · · ′ · ‾ ·
    he appreciated
    they participated

Possessives

1. ‾ ′
    my friend
    his watch
    our store
    their car
    your home

2. ‾ ′ ·
    my brother
    our parents
    his picture
    her glasses
    your lesson

3. ‾ ′ ‾
    my notebook
    their farmhouse
    our high school
    his rowboat
    your birthplace

4. ‾ ′ · ‾ ·
    her flower garden
    our dancing partners
    their science teacher
    his tennis racquet
    your station wagon

Practice Sentences

1. Shē's mȳ friénd.
2. Īt's thēir fármhoùse.
3. Thēy're hīs párents.
4. Hē's mȳ scíence tēacher.
5. Hē's ōur proféssor.

6. Īt's mȳ ōccupátion.
7. Īt's hēr wrístwàtch.
8. Īt's yōur túrn.
9. Shē's mȳ tèacher.
10. Īt's ōur hígh schōol.

Titles

1. ‾ ′
    Miss Jones
    Miss Hall

2. ‾ ′ •
    Miss Baker
    Miss Porter

3. ‾ ′ • •
    Miss Hamilton
    Miss Sheridan

4. ‾ • ′
    Mr. Black
    Mrs. Young
    Dr. Smith

5. ‾ • ′ •
    Mr. Griffith
    Mrs. Harris
    Dr. Parker

6. ‾ • ′ • •
    Mr. Harrison
    Mrs. Robinson
    Dr. Emery

7. ‾ • • ′ •
    Mr. Rinaldi
    Mrs. Santini
    Dr. McCallum

8. ‾ • ′ ‾
    Mr. Ridgeway
    Mrs. Warfield
    Dr. Skidmore

9. ‾ • • ′
    President Taft
    General Kim
    Admiral White

10. ‾ • • ′ •
    President Johnson
    President Hoover

11. ‾ • • ′ • •
    President Kennedy
    President Jefferson

Prepositions

1. ‾ ′
    in class
    in time
    in school
    at home
    at noon
    at work
    by bus
    by train
    by car
    with John
    for Bill

2. ‾ ′ •
    by taxi
    by letter
    for Helen
    for Henry
    with Mary

3. ‾ ′ ‾
    by airplane
    on horseback
    by steamship
    by streetcar

Drill A

Where's *Mr. Hárris?*

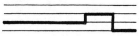

| Mr. Johnson |
| Mr. Elson |
| Dr. Parker |
| Mr. Wilson |

Hē's *īn cláss*

| in class |
| at school |
| at work |
| at home |

Drill B

Are you going *bȳ bús*?

| by bus |
| by train |
| by plane |
| by car |
| by boat |

Drill C

Ėxcúse mē   Āre yōu *Mȳss Jónes*?

Miss Jones	Mr. Blakely	General Jones
Miss White	Mrs. Wilson	President Smith
Miss Brown	Dr. Parker	Admiral Green

Modals and Auxiliaries

These include: be, have, can, could, may, might, shall, will, would, should, must.

**In Questions* (all modals and auxiliaries)

1.
Can he come?
Was she here?
Must you go?
Did you know?

2.
Are they coming?
Is she going?
Are you reading?
Were they trying?

3.
Do you remember?
Are they arriving?
Have you forgotten?
Were they agreeing?

4.
Is she studying?
Are you listening?
Are they worrying?
Is he bicycling?

In Affirmative Statements (all modals and auxiliaries except *be* and *can*)

5.
We should go.
You must come.
I shall try.
You may go.

6.
We must study.
I might worry.
You should study.
I will listen.

*The use of tertiary stress on both an auxiliary or modal and a following subject pronoun is not common, and is perhaps used only in rather careful, deliberate speech. This combination is usually spoken with vowel reductions, the loss of /h/ from *he*, and with tertiary-weak stress, or with weak-tertiary, and sometimes with weak-weak stress. *Can he come?* /kǽniy kə́m/, /kən hȳy kə́m/, /kə̀niy kə́m/. Some practice with these stress combinations and with vowel reductions is given in Sections 8 and 11.

Drill A

Can she come?	Yes, she can.
Did they go?	Yes, they did.
Was he here?	Yes, he was.
Have they gone?	Yes, they have.
May we go?	Yes, you may.

Special Expressions

Practice the expressions below until you can say them perfectly.

1. Good morning.
   Good evening.

2. Good night.
   Good-bye.

3. Good afternoon.

4. How are you?

5. Fine, thank you.

   How are you?

6. See you tomorrow.

Weak Stress

The Modal *can*

When used before verbs in affirmative statements, *can* is spoken with weak stress. *Can* is pronounced /kən/; it is never pronounced /kæn/ before a verb unless it is spoken that way for emphasis.

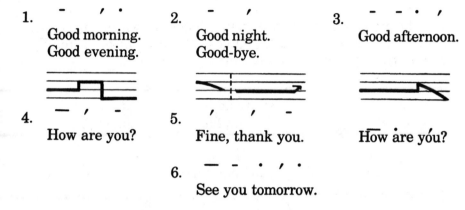

1. I can go
   he can swim
   you can try

2. you can answer
   she can study
   they can listen

3. he can forget
   they can begin
   she can reply

4. you can continue
   they can remember
   we can examine

5. we can broadcast
   they can translate
   he can export

be—Main Verb or Auxiliary (*am, is, are, was, were*)

In affirmative statements the forms of *be* are almost always spoken with weak stress, and often with a change in the vowel. *Are*, for example, is usually pronounced /ər/ rather than /ar/.

When speaking, of course, contractions are much more commonly used than the full forms of *be*. *We're coming* /wĭr kə́miŋ/ is more common than *We are coming* /wĭy ər kə́miŋ/.

1.   ‾ ∙   /
   I am John
   he was here
   they were here

2.   ‾ ∙   / ∙
   I am coming
   they are working
   he is waiting

3.   ‾ ∙   / ∙ ∙
   she is traveling
   we were wondering
   he was worrying

4.   ‾ ∙   ∙ / ∙
   she is beginning
   they were deciding
   we were preparing

5.   ‾   ∙   /   ‾ ∙
   they were broadcasting
   we were translating
   he was exporting

6.   ‾   ∙   / ∙ ‾ ∙
   she was telephoning
   he was operating
   we were classifying

The Pronoun *it*

When used after a verb, the pronoun *it* is almost always pronounced with weak stress, and it is usually pronounced as if it were a final syllable of the verb. Listen carefully to the examples and imitate them as closely as you can.

1.   / ∙
   do it
   read it
   try it
   find it
   write it

2.   / ∙ ∙
   study it
   finish it
   doing it
   reading it
   finished it

3.   / ∙∙ ∙
   studying it
   finishing it
   answering it
   questioning it
   publishing it

4.   ∙ /   ∙
   pronounce it
   forget it
   erase it
   report it
   exchange it

5.   ∙ / ∙ ∙
   remember it
   consider it
   completing it
   divided it
   decided it

6.   ∙/ ∙ ∙ ∙
   continuing it
   remembering it
   examining it
   considering it
   imagining it

7.   / ∙ ‾ ∙
   emphasized it
   realized it
   operates it

8.   / ∙ ∙ ‾ ∙ ∙
   emphasizing it
   realizes it
   separated it

9.   ∙   / ∙‾ ∙
   appreciates it

10.   ∙ / ∙‾ ∙ ∙
   appreciated it

11.   ‾ ∙   / ∙
   recommend it

12.   ‾ ∙   / ∙ ∙
   recommended it

Short sentences with *it*

1.   ‾ / ∙
   He did it.
   We saw it.
   She wants it.
   I heard it.

2.   ‾ / ∙ ∙
   We studied it.
   They've finished it.
   She's reading it.
   He's doing it.

3.   ‾ ∙ / ∙
   I forgot it.
   I can do it.
   She erased it.
   You can try it.

4.   ‾   ∙ / ∙ ∙
   They've completed it.
   I can finish it.
   He remembers it.
   We are doing it.

5.   ‾ ∙ / ∙ ∙
   He is studying it.
   She is answering it.
   They are finishing it.
   We are practicing it.

6.   ‾ / ∙ ‾   ∙
   I realized it.
   We emphasized it.
   They memorized it.
   He multiplied it.

Drill A

· · /·	— - /
Can you do it?	Yes, I can.
Will you try it?	Yes, I will.
Would he buy it?	Yes, he would.
Did she find it?	Yes, she did.
Have you done it?	Yes, I have.
May I read it?	Yes, you may.
Should we write it?	Yes, you should.
Does he know it?	Yes, he does.
Has she typed it?	Yes, she has.

Drill B

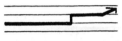

Hāve yōu *sóld it?*

/ ·	/ · ·	· / · ·
done it	written it	forgotten it
read it	studied it	remembered it
seen it	finished it	considered it
bought it	driven it	completed it
tried it	eaten it	decided it

Articles—*a, an, the, some*

1. · · /
    a book
    a pen
    an ear
    an egg
    the school
    the earth
    some soup
    some fruit

2. · / ·
    a pencil
    a table
    an apple
    an orange
    the paper
    the engine
    some glasses
    some sugar

3. · / · ·
    a formula
    a theater
    an elephant
    an animal
    the director
    the accident
    some articles
    some furniture

4. · · /
    a machine
    the guitar
    a surprise
    the parade

5. · · / ·
    a banana
    a tomato
    the eraser
    some equipment

6. · · / · ·
    a discovery
    an experience
    the experiment
    some Bolivians

Below are examples of articles before nouns with a tertiary stress, and before noun compounds.

7.   • ′ —
an athlete
some contracts
a railroad
the schoolboys

8.   • ′ • —
an exercise
the telephone
some tennis balls
a grammar book

9.   • ′ • — •
a dictionary
some territory
the flower garden
some writing paper

10.   • ′ • — • •
a movie theater
an army officer
some toilet articles
a traffic accident

11.   • • ′ • —
an aristocrat
a department store
an amusement park
some vanilla beans

12.   • ′ — •
a library
a typewriter
the bus driver
a school teacher

13.   •   • ′ • — •
some police equipment
the research department

14.   • • ′ •   — •
a detective story
the employment office

15.   •   — ′
some Chinese
the northeast
the fourteenth

16.   •   — • ′ •
some education
an invitation
the population

17.   • — • ′ • •
the university
an anniversary
an Ecuadorian

18.   • • — • ′ •
an examination
a communication
some appreciation

19.   • • — ′ •
an electrician

20.   • •   — • ′ • •
an encyclopedia

21.   • — •   • ′ •
a recommendation

22.   • •   — • ′ • •
an impossibility

23.   • — • ′ • • •
a conversationalist

Preposition — Article — Noun

1.   —   • ′
in the house
on the bus
at the store
in a car

2.   —   • ′ •
in the garden
in a minute
on the ceiling
for the doctor

3.   —   • ′ • •
on the calendar
in the hospital
at the theater

4.   —   • ′ • —
in the grammar book
in the summertime
in the dining room

5.   — • • ′ • —
in an election year
at the amusement park
in a discussion group

Practice Sentences

1. He's in the house.
2. She's in the kitchen.
3. They're in the classroom.
4. It's in the newspaper.
5. She was in the hospital.

6. We were in a shipwreck.
7. We were in a traffic accident.
8. She was at the beauty parlor.
9. He was in the barbershop.
10. They were in a discussion group.

5. WORD COMBINATION STRESS (2) MAJOR STRESS

(Tape 6 begins here)

Major stress refers to the stresses that are the strongest, loudest or most prominent. The two major stresses are primary and secondary stress.

There are certain classes of words that have major stress. These are: (1) *adjectives* (and other noun modifiers), (2) *verbs*, (3) *nouns*, (4) *adverbs*. If these words do not receive the primary stress of a phrase, then their primary word stress is reduced, usually to secondary stress. Syllables with secondary stress are spoken with slightly less force or loudness than those with primary stress. Syllables spoken with secondary stress are louder and slightly longer than those spoken with one of the minor stresses—tertiary or weak.

To indicate secondary stress we shall use a horizontal line that is longer than the line we use for tertiary stress. Here are a few examples:

> The book was long.   It was a long book.
> The car was black.   It's a black car.
> I can't come.   I can't come tonight.
> They are leaving.   They are leaving now.

We shall begin our practice with adjective-noun combinations.

Noun Modifiers

Adjectives and Numerals

1. — ′	2. — ′ •	3. — ′ • •
long road	long river	new furniture
big house	nice person	good company
black shoes	good sailor	large continent
five schools	black sweater	big elephant
large farm	one ticket	wild animal
two chairs	five towels	new theater
nine books	big office	fine hospital
dark room	good movie	fine furniture

4 — • ′ •	5. — • ′ • •	6. — ′ -	7. — ′ • -
good mechanic	good ability	good athlete	long boulevard
wrong direction	long experiment	fine program	white telephone
two physicians	new discovery	bad contract	large hemisphere
new equipment	white thermometer	good income	new diplomat
old explorer	good experience	bad insult	long exercise

Practice Sentences

1. He's a nīce pérson.
   He's a good sailor.
   It's a long river.

2. It's a fāst tráin.
   He's a tall boy.
   She's a fine girl.

3. It's a fīne hóspital.

4. He's a good mechánic.

5. It was a new discóvery.

6. It was a lōng éxercise.

7. We were on a lārge fárm.

8. It was good éxperience.

The next group has adjectives of more than one syllable.

8. ‾ • ⁄
   cloudy day
   hungry boy
   modern house
   seven books
   yellow car
   thirsty child

9. ‾ • ⁄ •
   happy person
   seven houses
   sunny weather
   older brother
   youngest sister
   twenty people

10. ‾ • ⁄ • •
   modern furniture
   biggest continent
   hungry animal
   quiet hospital
   useful articles
   seven visitors

11. • ‾ • ⁄
   important book
   exciting place
   delightful child
   attractive house
   convenient place

12. • ‾ • ⁄ •
   amusing story
   delightful people
   important lessons
   exciting movie
   confusing lesson

13. • ‾ • • ⁄ •
   important department
   exciting conclusion
   amusing example
   confusing discovery
   convenient appointment

14. ‾ • • ⁄
   favorite book
   beautiful child
   opposite way
   marvelous road
   excellent school

15. ‾ • • ⁄ •
   possible answer
   marvelous weather
   excellent sailor
   difficult language
   favorite picture

16. ‾ • • • ⁄ •
   possible condition
   marvelous adventures
   opposite direction
   beautiful piano
   favorite amusement

Nouns and participles can also modify nouns.

17. ‾ ⁄
   gold watch
   wool suit
   brick house
   March rain
   glass door
   cooked meat
   fried eggs
   paid bill

18. ‾ • ⁄
   cotton dress
   leather shoes
   summer coat
   winter hat
   summer rain
   falling snow
   singing bird
   broken dish

19. ‾ • ⁄ •
   winter weather
   linen napkin
   cotton stockings
   broken dishes
   golden slippers
   lettuce salad
   open window
   married daughter

20. • ‾ • ⁄ •
   Atlantic Ocean

21. ‾ • ⁄ • •
   city government

22. ‾ • ⁄ • •
   state economy

23. ‾ • ⁄ •
   school diploma

24. ‾ • • - • ⁄ • •
   Washington University

25. - ‾ • • ⁄ •
   unfurnished apartment

The examples here are of adjectives and numerals modifying noun compounds.

1. — · ́ -
biggest high school
twenty classrooms
happy schoolboy
heavy raincoat

2. — · ́ · -
easy grammar book
oldest weatherman
pleasant living room
yellow fountain pen

3. — · ́ - ·
biggest fire engine
oldest newspaper
empty wastebasket
smallest typewriter

4. — · ́ · - ·
pretty flower garden
newest filling station
oldest fairy stories
finest writing paper

5. — · · ́ -
wonderful highway
excellent wristwatch
favorite classroom

6. · — · ́ · -
important grammar book
delightful summertime
convenient parking place

7. · — · ́ - ·
important newspaper
attractive post office
convenient gas station

8. · — · ́ · - ·
delightful flower garden
convenient filling station
exciting horror story

9. — ́ -
five textbooks
six houseguests
eight blackbirds
four test tubes

10. - — ́ - ·
eighteen racehorses
sixteen matchfolders
fourteen school buses
nineteen mailboxes

Practice Sentences

1. It was a cloudy day.
2. It's an important book.
3. She is a delightful child.
4. It was an attractive house.
5. It's an amusing story.
6. It is an exciting movie.
7. It was a difficult assignment.
8. It was an easy grammar book.
9. There were seven traffic accidents.
10. It's her new sewing machine.

There are a few interesting cases in English where the same combination of words is used both as a noun compound and as a modified noun structure. The noun compounds have all developed specialized meanings.

1. dark róom   (a room that is dark)
   dárkroom   (special room used in photography)

2. green hóuse   (a house that is green)
   gréenhouse   (a glass structure used for growing plants)

3. black bírd   (any bird that is black)
   bláckbird   (a particular kind of bird)

4. blue bird   (any bird that is blue)
    bluebird   (a particular kind of bird)

5. black board (a long piece of wood that is black in color)
    blackboard   (a large slate used for writing with chalk)

6. light house (a house that lets in a lot of light, or that is painted with a light color)
    lighthouse   (a tall tower with a light for warning ships)

7. white house (a house that is white in color)
    White House (the residence of the President of the U.S.)

In the examples above, the difference is indicated in the writing system by writing the noun compounds as one word (except White House) and the other combinations as two words. This is not a reliable guide, however, as many noun compounds are written as two words. Here are a few examples:

Noun Compounds

Written as one word	*Written as two words*
farmhouse	farm hand
schoolboy	school board
wristband	wrist watch

The only reliable guide to noun compounds is the stress combination of primary-tertiary stress.

Practice Sentences

These sentences use the noun compounds and word combinations above.

1. We went in the green house.
2. We went in the greenhouse.
3. He's in the darkroom.
4. Not all dark rooms are darkrooms.
5. He lives in the white house.
6. He doesn't live in the White House.
7. We need a black board.
8. We need a blackboard.
9. I've seen many black birds.
10. I've never seen a blackbird.

Exercise

In this exercise decide whether your teacher, or the voice on tape, is saying A or B in each group.

1. A. redbird (a special kind of bird)
    B. red bird (any bird that is red)

2. A. cheapskates (people that are stingy)
    B. cheap skates (inexpensive skates)

3. A. yellowjacket (a wasp, or bee-like insect)
    B. yellow jacket (a yellow coat)

4. A. lóngbōat (a particular kind of boat)
   B. lōng bóat (any boat that is long)

5. A. hót plāte (an electric cooking device)
   B. hōt pláte (any plate that is hot)

6. A. hárdbāll (a baseball)
   B. hārd báll (any ball that is hard)

7. A. bíg tōp (another name for a circus tent)
   B. bīg tóp (a top that is big)

8. A. Hē's īn thė gréenhŏuse.
   B. Hē's īn thė grēen hóuse.

9. A. Wē sāw sŏme bláckbīrds.
   B. Wē sāw sŏme blāck bírds.

10. A. Dō yŏu nēed ȧ bláckbōard?
    B. Dō yŏu nēed ȧ blāck bóard?

11. A. Hē dŏesn't līke dárkrŏoms.
    B. Hē dŏesn't līke dārk róoms.

12. A. Hē līves īn thė líghthŏuse.
    B. Hē līves īn thė līght hóuse.

13. A. Ī sāw ȧ rédbīrd.
    B. Ī sāw ȧ rēd bírd.

14. A. Wē thōught thēy wėre chéapskātes.
    B. Wē thōught thēy wėre chēap skátes.

15. A. Ī sāw ȧ yéllowjăckėt.
    B. Ī sāw ȧ yēllow jáckėt.

16. A. Thēy wėre īn ȧ lóngbōat.
    B. Thēy wėre īn ȧ lōng bóat.

17. A. Hē līves īn thė Whīte Hōuse.
    B. Hē līves īn thė whīte hóuse.

18. A. Hē pīcked ūp thė hót plāte.
    B. Hē pīcked ūp thė hōt pláte.

19. A. Hāve yŏu ēvėr sēen ȧ hórseflȳ?
    (a particular kind of fly)
    B. Hāve yŏu ēvėr sēen ȧ hōrse flý?
    (a horse that is able to fly)

20. A. Hāve yŏu ēvėr sēen ȧ bóardwālk?
    (a wooden walkway along the seashore)

B. Have you ever seen a board walk?
(a piece of wood that is able to walk)

Verbs

Verb-Noun Object

1.

play cards
write books
see John
help June

2.

playing cards
writing books
study French
visit friends

3.

writing letters
painting pictures
eating breakfast
studies English

4.

buy some ice skates
had a toothache
bought a toothbrush
wrote a textbook

5.

reads the newspaper
had a typewriter
found the timetable
fixed the light fixture

6.

forgot the appointment
begin an assignment
attend a convention
select a companion

7.

bought some playing cards
wants a pocket knife

8.

brought some farm equipment
called the fire department

9.

had a dental appointment
bought some smoking tobacco

10.

saw the filling station
had some swimming practice

Practice Sentences (1)

1. He is playing cards.
2. They are speaking French.
3. They are writing letters.
4. She is eating breakfast.
5. He is studying French.
6. They are visiting friends.
7. We bought some ice skates.
8. He had a toothache.

9. They realized the difficulty.
10. I bought some playing cards.
11. They called the fire department.
12. I had a dental appointment.
13. She was reading the newspaper.
14. You have a telephone call.
15. He emptied the wastebasket.

Practice Sentences (2)

1. We saw a good movie.
2. She bought a black sweater.
3. We crossed a long river.
4. He read a good book.
5. She bought some black shoes.

6. We took a long vacation.
7. I found a black umbrella.
8. We read an amusing story.
9. They saw an exciting movie.

Practice Sentences (3)

1. They līve īn a bīg hóuse.
2. We went on a fast train.
3. He lives on a large farm.
4. We went on a long walk.
5. Hē wōrks īn a bīg óffice.
6. We live in a big city.
7. Thēy trāveled ōn a fāst pláne.

8. Hē gōes tō thē nēw hígh schōol.
9. Thēy gōt īn thē nēarest lifebōat.
10. Shē wōrks īn thē nēw téxtile mīll.

Drill

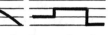

Hāve yōu rēad thē bóok?
Hāve yōu sēen thē móvie?
Dīd yōu stūdy thē lésson?
Hāve yōu hēard thē néws?
Dīd yōu wrīte thē létter?
Cān yōu hēar thē músic?
Dīd yōu fīnd yōur wátch?
Hāve yōu fīnished yōur wórk?

Yés. Ī've réad it.
Yés. Ī've séen it.
Yés. Ī stúdied it.
Yés. Ī've héard it.
Yés. Ī wróte it.
Yés. Ī cån héar it.
Yés. Ī fóund it.
Yés. Ī've fínished it.

Verb-Adverb

1.   —   /
   come here
   go there
   sign here
   read fast

2.   —   • /
   come again
   leave tonight
   try again
   go today

3.   —• • /
   do it again
   leaving tonight
   try it again
   saw it today

4.   — / • •
   work carefully
   come frequently
   spoke angrily
   drive carefully

5.   — / •
   run quickly
   go slowly
   come often
   eat early

6.   —• /
   try it now
   study hard
   find it soon
   doing fine

7.   —• / •
   eating early

8.   • —• • / •
   arriving tomorrow

9.   —• • / • •
   listen carefully

10.   — • • / •• •
   come immediately

Practice Sentences

1. S͞ign hére.
2. C͞ome agáin
3. Dr͞ive slówly.
4. D͞o it nów.
5. Lìsten cárefùlly.
6. Tr͞y it agáin.
7. Th͞ey e͞at éarly.

8. Hē's c͞oming tonìght.
9. Th͞ey c͞ome fréquèntly.
10. W͞e càn f͞inish éasily.
11. Th͞ey àre l͞eaving tomórròw.
12. Shē's c͞oming āt n͞ine o'clóck.
13. Th͞ey càn c͞ome āt t͞en o'clóck.
14. Ī forg͞ot it agáin.

The Word — *not*   *(Tape 7 begins here)*

1. `-  —  ′  ·`
He's not coming.
They're not swimming.
I'm not going.
We're not leaving.
You're not trying.

2. `- ·  —  ′  ·`
He is not coming.
They are not swimming.
I am not going.
We are not leaving.
You are not trying.

Negative Contractions (*can't, isn't, don't, wouldn't,* etc.)

1. `—  ′`
don't go
can't come
won't leave
won't come

2. `—  ′ ·`
aren't coming
can't see it
won't do it
don't like it

3. `— ·  ′`
doesn't know
didn't try
shouldn't go
couldn't swim

4. `— · ′ ·`
couldn't do it
wasn't leaving
didn't know it

5. `— · · ′ ·`
doesn't remember
isn't arriving
wouldn't continue

6. `—  ′ · ·`
weren't listening
aren't finishing
weren't studying

Practice Sentences (1)

1. D͞on't gó.
2. D͞on't dó it.
3. Hē's n͞ot cóming.
4. Th͞ey w͞on't léave.
5. Sh͞e wóuldn't dó it.

6. H͞e d͞idn't remémbèr.
7. H͞e h͞asn't télephōned.
8. Ī d͞on't ùnderstánd.
9. Sh͞e d͞idn't appréciàte it.
10. H͞e d͞oesn't remémbèr it.

Practice Sentences (2)

1. Can't he cóme?
2. Won't they dó it?
3. Didn't she remémber?
4. Wouldn't they lísten?
5. Shouldn't you télephōne?
6. Isn't she stúdying?

Practice Sentences (3)

1. We can't leave tonight.
2. Don't do it agáin.
3. You didn't listen cárefully.
4. They won't leave tomórrow.
5. She can't come at nine o'clóck.

Practice Sentences (4)

1. We haven't seen the latest móvie.
2. I haven't read today's néwspaper.
3. She doesn't eat a late bréakfast.
4. I don't need a new tóothbrush.
5. They didn't réalize the difficulty.

The Word—*please*

1.   ⎯   ′
   Please come.
   Please go.
   Please try.

2.   ⎯   ′·
   Please do it.
   Please find it.
   Please buy it.

3.   ⎯   · ′ ·
   Please remember.
   Please continue.
   Please confirm it.

4.   ⎯   ⎯   ′
   Please don't go.
   Please don't talk.
   Please don't run.

5.   ⎯   ⎯   · ′
   Please don't forget.
   Please don't return.
   Please don't begin.

Practice Sentences

1. Please try hárder.
2. Please come tomorrow mórning.
3. Please continue your wórk.
4. Please don't stóp.
5. Please don't run in the hálls.
6. Please don't buy an expénsive wátch.
7. Please don't lose your new ríng.
8. Please don't forget your néwspaper.
9. Please don't talk to the óperātor.
10. Please don't walk on the gráss.

Nouns

Nouns as subjects

1.   — ′

Birds sing.
John knows.
Ed's here.

2.   — · ′

John's a boy.
June's a girl.
Jeff's a child.

3.   — · ′·

Bill is writing.
June can do it
Bob is coming.

4.   · — · ′

The books are here.
The clock is wrong.

5.   — · · ′

Sugar is sweet.
Tennis is fun.

6.   — · · ′ ·

English is easy.
Children are noisy.

7.   · — · · ′

The razor is sharp.
The office is closed.

8.   · — · · ′ ·

The flower is pretty.
The window is open.

9.   · — · ′ · ·

The play was excellent.
The show was wonderful.

10.   - · — · · ′

Mister Taylor is tall.
Mrs. Johnson is short.

11.   — · · · ′ · ·

Medicine is wonderful.
Africa is beautiful.

Practice Sentences

1. The wind blew.
2. The children cried.
3. The river was long.
4. The package arrived.
5. The weather is cold.
6. The car was new.
7. The musician played.
8. The sweater was beautiful.
9. The audience laughed.
10. The towel was wet.
11. Education is important.
12. The engineer came.
13. Miss Jones understood.
14. The cafeteria is open.

Names

1.   — ′

John Smith
Phil White
Jeff Hall

2.   — · ′

Mary Jones
Helen Black
Alan Stone

3.   — · ′ ·

Betty Cooper
Bobby Sheeler
Ellie Hoffman

4.   — · — · ′

Roger Henry Jones
Richard Franklin Gray
Herbert Thomas Hand

5.   — · — · ′ ·

John Fernandez Thomas
James Rinaldi Collins
June McCallum Rogers

Initials are also used, of course. They, too, have secondary stress.

6.   — — ′ ·

John A. Roberts
June J. Johnson

7.   — — ′

A. A. Fair
H. B. Downs

People are sometimes referred to just by their initials. Newspapers frequently do this when referring to famous people.

8.

F. D. R.	(Franklin Delano Roosevelt)
J. F. K.	(John Fitzgerald Kennedy)
L. B. J.	(Lyndon Baines Johnson)

Practice Sentences

1. His name is John A. Floyd.
2. Helen Black is coming to the party.
3. Richard Henry Green is his full name.
4. F. D. R. refers to Franklin Delano Roosevelt.
5. This book was written by A. A. Fair.

Noun Compounds as subjects

1. The classrooms are large.
2. The grocery store is open.
3. The bus driver arrived.
4. The ink bottle is empty.
5. The movie theater is closed.
6. Steel production has improved.
7. The farm equipment arrived.
8. The swimming pool is closed.
9. The newspaper hasn't come.
10. The playing cards are in the desk.

Question Words

Question words such as *who, what, when, why, how, where* usually have secondary stress.

1. When is he coming?
2. When did you arrive?
3. Who is your English teacher?
4. Where did you lose your watch?
5. Why can't you come?
6. How is your wife?
7. What does he want?
8. Where do you work?
9. When did you finish the lesson?
10. Why didn't Mrs. Jones buy a new dress?

Drill

When are you leaving?	Tomorrow.
Where are you going?	To Chicago.
Where is your father?	In the house.
Who is that lady?	That's Mrs. Johnson.
When did you see him?	Last Saturday.
Where's my notebook?	On the table.

Practice Sentences — Review (1)

1. The gold watch was new.
2. Those houses are old.
3. The summer rains arrived.
4. John can't go.
5. The teacher won't like it.
6. The doctor couldn't come.
7. Mary couldn't swim.
8. Miss Taylor didn't understand.
9. Miss Jones hasn't taught.
10. The mechanic couldn't fix it.
11. I speak English.
12. She was reading a magazine.
13. Dr. Smith couldn't come.
14. Please don't forget.
15. Her new sweater was nice.
16. The grocery store is closed.
17. I don't like winter weather.
18. Your summer coat is in the closet.
19. They live in a brick house.
20. He has a dental appointment.

Practice Sentences — Review (2)

Now read these sentences. Only the primary stress of the phrase is marked.

1. They are leaving tomorrow.
2. He hasn't telephoned.
3. They won't come.
4. Please don't stop.
5. English is easy.
6. Education is important.
7. It was good experience.
8. She's wearing a cotton dress.
9. It's an amusing story.
10. They are visiting friends.
11. Drive carefully.
12. Don't do it.
13. We went early.
14. Please don't forget your book.
15. His television set is new.
16. Your book is on the desk.
17. Mrs. Johnson can't come.
18. The children were crying.
19. When are you coming?
20. Call the fire department.

6. INTONATION (1)

Declarative Intonation

(Tape 8 begins here)

The two most common intonation patterns are (1) the declarative and (2) the question intonation.

We have had practice with both kinds of intonation patterns in previous parts of the book. You will recall that the declarative intonation begins on pitch level 2, rises to pitch 3, and then either steps down or glides down to pitch 1. The voice steps down if one or more syllables follow the primary stress of the phrase; otherwise it glides down. We can also call the declarative intonation the /231/ pattern. The /231/ intonation pattern is used in affirmative and negative statements, and in questions beginning with a question word. Here are a few review sentences.

When are you cóming?
What is he doing?
Why are they going?
Where is your brother?

June is my sister.
Bill is my brother.

It is possible to say many sentences in two phrases. Listen to the following sentences which are said in two ways. We shall use a vertical dotted line to show the division between phrases in the column to the right.

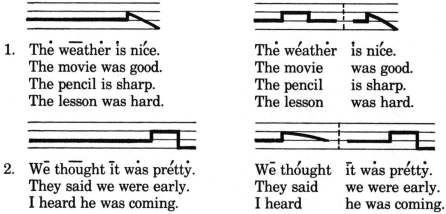

1. The weather is níce.   The wéather   is níce.
    The movie was good.   The movie   was good.
    The pencil is sharp.   The pencil   is sharp.
    The lesson was hard.   The lesson   was hard.

2. We thought it was prétty.   We thóught   it was prétty.
    They said we were early.   They said   we were early.
    I heard he was coming.   I heard   he was coming.

48

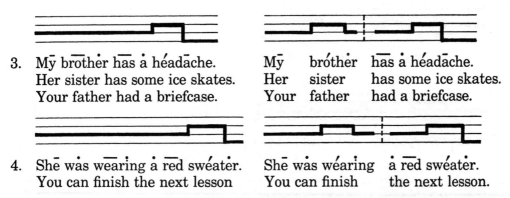

3. My brŏthĕr hās ȧ héadāche.
    Her sister has some ice skates.
    Your father had a briefcase.

    My   brŏthĕr hās ȧ héadāche.
    Her   sister   has some ice skates.
    Your   father   had a briefcase.

4. Shē wȧs wēaring ȧ réd swéatĕr.
    You can finish the next lesson

    Shē wȧs wéaring ȧ rēd swéatĕr.
    You can finish   the next lesson.

There are two important things to know about sentences that are spoken with two or more phrases:

(1) Each phrase has one — and only one — primary stress.

(2) The sound of the voice does not actually stop between phrases.

There is the slightest kind of hesitation, but the sound of the voice continues. This kind of hesitation has been called "a shifting of gears."

Notice in the sentences above with two phrases that at the end of the first phrase, the voice does not actually go down to the pitch 1 level, but rather comes down only to the 2 level. The second phrase is /231/, identical with the basic declarative intonation pattern you have been practicing. The two phrase intonation pattern can be called the declarative compound pattern, or the declarative 2 pattern, or it can be simply referred to as the /232ᐟ231/ pattern.

This kind of intonation pattern is extremely common, and it is used with sentences that have two phrases joined by a connecting word such as *and, but, or*. These connecting words have weak or tertiary stress. Below are some sentences of this kind for practice.

Practice Sentences (1)

1. Bīll cȧn wríte,   būt hē cān't spéll.
    Jim can swim,   but he can't dive.
    John can see,   but he can't hear.

2. Ī ate thė fóod,   bȧt Ī wāsn't húngry.

3. Ī rēad thė bóok,   bȧt Ī dīdn't líke ȧt.

4. Ī māde ȧn appóintmėnt,   bȧt Ī dīdn't kéep ȧt.

5. Thė reāson fŏr thė delāy wāsn't gíven.

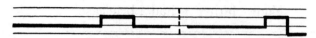

6. Ĭt wăs īn thė néwspāpėr,   bŭt Ĭ dīdn't sée ĭt.

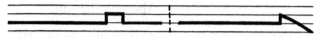

7. Wē wėre īn ăn áccidėnt,   bŭt wē wēren't húrt.

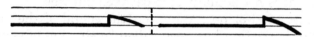

8. Ĭ wāitėd fŏr ăn hóur,   bŭt Jōhn dīdn't cóme.

9. Hĭs nāme ĭs Jóhn ănd hē līves ĭn Fránce.

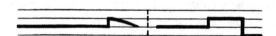

10. Ĭt wăs ă gōod bóok,   ānd Ĭ ėnjóyed ĭt.

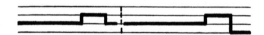

11. Ĭ lōst thė tíckėt ănd cōuldn't fínd ĭt.

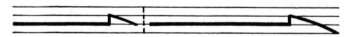

12. Wē wēnt dŏwntówn ănd bōught sŏme nēw clóthes.

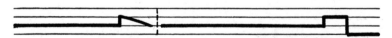

13. Hē līves ĭn Nēw Yórk ānd wōrks āt thė Ūnītėd Nátions.

14. Hē ėnjōys hĭs wórk ănd hē līkes Nēw Yórk.

Practice Sentences (2)

Read the sentences below with the same intonation you have been practicing.

1. It was a long éxercīse, but I fínished it.
2. I stūdied the lésson, but I dīdn't remémber it.
3. The food wasn't góod, but I áte it.
4. It wāsn't éasy, but I díd it.
5. I drōve the cár, but I was cáreful.
6. I was tíred and wēnt to béd.
7. Hē was láte and mīssed his bús.
8. Hē's nōt Énglish, and hē's nōt Frénch.
9. I hāve twō sísters, and hē hās four bróthers.
10. Hē lēaves āt níne, and retūrns āt fíve.
11. Hē jōined a círcus and trāveled tō Eúrope.
12. Hē wēnt tō the ópera, and sāw a fīne perfórmance.

Practice Sentences (3)

Read the sentences below. Only the primary stress of each phrase is marked.

1. I know Jóhn, but I don't know Bíll.
2. We saw the móvie, but we didn't líke it.
3. It was her bírthday, and I bought a nice gíft.
4. He speaks Énglish, but he doesn't speak Chinése.
5. I read bóoks, but I don't read mágazines.
6. He looks at télevision, but he doesn't líke it.
7. I went to the lécture, but I didn't understánd it.
8. She went to the stóre and bought some gróceries.
9. He wrote the létter, but he never máiled it.
10. We went to the méeting and had a good tíme.

Direct Address

When a term of direct address is used, the sentence is spoken in two phrases. The first phrase has the /232/ intonation; the second phrase is usually on the pitch 2 level with a slight rise at the end.

Listen to these sentences:

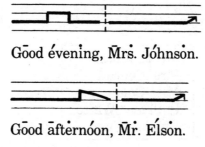

Gōod évening, Mrs. Jóhnson.

Gōod aftérnóon, Mr. Élson.

How do you dó, Mr. Wílson?

Good-býe, Dr. Nélson.

Drill A

Good mórning, *Bill.*

| Jane |
| Mr. White |
| Mrs. Black |
| Dr. Jones |
| Miss Smith |

Drill B

Good évening, *Bób.*

| June |
| Mr. Edwards |
| Dr. Jones |
| Miss Nelson |
| Professor Smith |
| General |

It is also possible to say the name on the pitch 1 level. When we do this, it is more formal.

Drill C

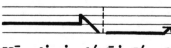

How do you dó, *Dr. Jónes?*

| Mr. Hoffman |
| Mrs. Conrad |
| Miss Cole |
| Professor White |
| Dr. Whitman |

Drill D

I'm glad to know you, *Miss Green.*

> Mrs. Smith
> Mr. Brown
> Dr. Westfield
> Phillip
> Barbara

If the name appears first, it is said as follows:

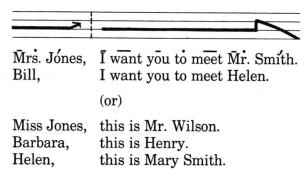

Mrs. Jónes,   I want you to meet Mr. Smith.
Bill,   I want you to meet Helen.

(or)

Miss Jones,   this is Mr. Wilson.
Barbara,   this is Henry.
Helen,   this is Mary Smith.

Questions with declarative intonation, directed to someone by name, have the intonation—/232¦2 ⤴/ or /232¦1 ⤴/

When are you léaving, Bíll?

Why did you dó it, Hénry?

What is your náme, little bóy?

Practice Sentences

1. When did you sée it, Bób?
2. Where did you héar it, Jáck?
3. Why couldn't you cóme, Bárbara?
4. When are you planning to stúdy, Júne?
5. What are you dóing, little gírl?

Affirmative and negative statements, directed to someone by name, also have the same basic intonation pattern /232:2 ˙ ˈ/

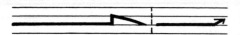

1. I hope you can cóme, Mīss Jónes.
2. Mother needs your hélp, Hárriet.
3. I don't knów, Dr. Smíth.
4. She wants to knów, Hérbert.
5. We don't remémber, Mrs. Jóhnson.

Contrast Drill

In this drill, the sentences in the left column have a name as the direct object of the verb. The sentences in the right-hand column have names used in direct address.

1. We haven't met Máry.   We haven't mét,   Máry.

2. I don't know Miss Jónes.   I don't knów,   Miss Jónes.

3. He doesn't remember Máry.   He doesn't remémber,   Máry.

4. I can't hear Jóhn.   I can't héar,   Jóhn.

5. I'll never forget Hénry.   I'll never forgét,   Hénry.

6. I haven't written móther.   I haven't wrítten,   Móther.

7. She hasn't called Bárbara.   She hasn't cálled,   Bárbara.

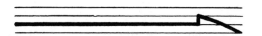 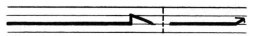

8. Thē chīldrĕn cān't sēe Mĭss Whíte.   Thē chīldrĕn cān't sée,   Mĭss Whíte.

Exercise

In this exercise you are asked to listen to the sentences below and decide whether they are like the sentence in Column 1 (name used as object of the verb with declarative intonation /231/); or whether they are like the sentence in Column 2 (name used as a term of direct address, with intonation 232|2 ⤴ /)

We have written the sentences without stress marks and commas. You will have to listen in order to decide.

	Column 1 *I can't see Mary.*	Column 2 *I can't see, Mary.*
1. I don't know Mr. Jones.		
2. John doesn't remember Helen.		
3. I haven't written mother.		
4. She hasn't called Mary.		
5. I couldn't hear Dr. Jones.		
6. We haven't met Miss Smith.		
7. I haven't forgotten Professor Johnson.		
8. I haven't heard Bill.		
9. He doesn't remember Miss Black.		
10. We don't know Dr. Smith.		

Question Intonation

This is the second of the two most common intonation patterns. You will recall that the question begins on pitch 2 level, then steps up to pitch 3 level, and then either steps up or glides to a slightly higher position. This intonation pattern is used with questions that begin with a modal or auxiliary. Here are a few examples:

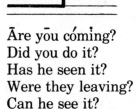

Āre yōu cóming?
Did you do it?
Has he seen it?
Were they leaving?
Can he see it?

Direct Address

When a term of address is used, the question is spoken in two phrases. The first phrase begins on pitch 2, rises to pitch 3; there is a very slight hesitation, and the second phrase begins on pitch 3 and ends with a slight rise. Listen to the examples below:

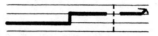

Āre yōu cóming, Bíll?
Are you leaving, Jim?
Did you study, June?
Have you finished, George?
Did you see it, Ed?
Can you do it, Jeff?

Practice Sentences

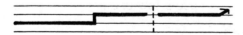

1.   Āre yŏu cóming, Móthèr?

2.   Āre yŏu hére, Máry?

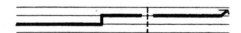

3.   Hāve yōu forgóttèn, Mīss Smíth?

4.   Dīd yōu sée ìt, Jéff?

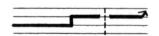

5.   Cān't yōu remémbèr, Mr. Wílsòn?

6.   Wīll yŏu hélp, Óffìcèr?

Drill A

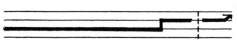

Hāve yōu fīnished yōur wórk, *Bíll?*

> John
> Helen
> Mr. Olson
> Mrs. Rice
> Miss Markham

Drill B

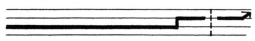

Māy Ī hēlp yōu wīth yōur cóat, *Jóhn?*

> Mr. Smith
> Mrs. Oliver
> Miss Green
> Dr. Denver
> sir

Practice Sentences

Read these sentences. Only the primary stress of each of the phrases is marked.

1. Have you read the néwspaper, Dád?
2. Did you find your wrístwatch, Mr. Gárvin?
3. Have you heard the néws, Hárriet?
4. Are you ready to gó, Móther?
5. Would you like some téa, Mrs. Nélson?
6. Have you seen the new móvie, Hélen?
7. Would you please help the téacher, Jóhn?
8. Do you know what it iś, dóctor?
9. Do you know the wáy, Mr. Jénkins?
10. Is this your new cóat, Bétty?

Contrast Drill

In this drill, the sentences in the left column have a name as the object of the verb. The sentences in the right column have names used in direct address.

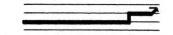   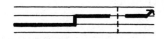

1. Āre yōu cālling Bíll?   Āre yōu cálling, Bíll?

2. Dĭd yōu cāll Júne?   Dĭd yōu cáll, Júne?

3. Cān yōu seē M̄rs. Jóhnsŏn?   Cān yōu sée, M̄rs. Jóhnsŏn?

4. Dĭd yōu hēlp D̄r. Whíte?   Dĭd yōu hélp, D̄r. Whíte?

5. Dĭd yōu ūndĕrstānd Bób?   Dĭd yōu ūndĕrstánd, Bób?

6. Āre yōu gōing tŏ wrīte Jóhn?   Āre yōu gōing tŏ wríte, Jóhn?

7. Dō yōu knōw M̄iss Bláck?   Dō yōu knów, M̄iss Bláck?

Exercise

In this exercise, listen to the sentences below and decide whether they are like the sentences in Column 1 or Column 2. No commas or stress marks are written in the sentences.

	Column 1 *Can you see Bill?*	Column 2 *Can you see, Bill?*
1. Do you remember Bill?		
2. Will you write Mother?		
3. Have you forgotten Miss Smith?		
4. Did you understand John?		
5. Do you remember Dr. Holmes?		
6. Do you know Miss Nelson?		
7. Can you hear Helen?		

8. Did you call Mary?

9. Will you help Jeff?

10. Have we met Mrs. Brown?

7. WORD COMBINATION STRESS (3) MAJOR STRESS

Adverbs *(Tape 9 begins here)*

Intensifiers

Intensifiers have secondary stress when they precede adjectives.

1. ▔ ′

quite nice
quite good
too long
too big

2. ▔ · ′

very hard
very nice
rather long
very good

3. ▔ · ′·

very quiet
rather easy
very angry
rather happy

4. · ▔ · ′

extremely good

5. · ▔ · · ′

exceedingly long

6. ▔ · · ′ · ·

terribly difficult

7. ▔ · ▔ · ′

very, very good

8. ▔ · ▔ · ′ · ·

very, very difficult

9. ▔ · ▔ · ′ ·

very, very funny

Practice Sentences

1. She is very pretty.
2. George works very hard.
3. It's quite nice.
4. The lesson was too easy.
5. It was rather difficult.
6. The movie was extremely good.
7. I thought it was very nice.
8. The play was exceedingly long.
9. The book was very, very good.
10. English is very, very easy.

Adverbs of Frequency

Adverbs of frequency generally come before verbs and have secondary stress.

1. ▔ · ′

often comes
seldom went
always works
never tries

2. ▔ · · · ′

usually asks
usually came
generally knows
generally find

3. ▔ - ′

sometimes goes
sometimes works
sometimes helps
sometimes find

With a form of the verb *be*, these adverbs come after the verb and before the adjective or adverb.

60

4. ‾ · ′   5. ‾ ·· ′   6. ‾ - ′

seldom true	usually late	sometimes late
never right	usually glad	sometimes true
often wrong	generally true	sometimes wrong
always sad	generally white	sometimes right

Practice Sentences

1. He is seldom wróng.
2. She is usually ríght.
3. We are never láte.
4. John is often éarly.
5. That's generally trúe.
6. Miss Johnson is sometimes cróss.
7. John usually wíns.

8. Bill often stúdies.
9. They seldom dríve.
10. They usually wálk.
11. We sometimes wórk.
12. She doesn't often síng.
13. Mr. White never cáme.
14. That's seldom trúe.

Verbs—Followed by *ing-form* of Another Verb

Certain verbs can be followed by the *ing-form* of another verb. In this case the verb preceding the *ing-form* is spoken with secondary stress.

1. ‾ ′ ·   2. · ‾ ′ ·   3. ‾ ′· ·

stop reading	enjoy walking	stop doing it
start counting	begin driving	start eating it
hate working	advise doing	hate washing it
like playing	delay going	fear hearing it

Practice Sentences with Pronoun Subject

1. He began dríving.
2. They stopped dóing it.
3. She likes gárdening.
4. We dislike héaring it.
5. We started cóunting it.

6. I don't like wórking.
7. They stopped exámining it.
8. We can't delay góing.
9. They began dáncing.
10. He doesn't enjoy wáiting.

Practice Sentences with Noun Subject

1. John finished éating.
2. Mrs. Johnson started dríving.
3. June began prácticing.
4. Jeff Stone finished stúdying.
5. Bill dislikes fíghting.

6. John hasn't finished wórking.
7. Bill won't stop sínging.
8. Mr. James doesn't enjoy wálking.
9. Miss White finished téaching.
10. Bobby dislikes wríting.

If a noun object comes after the *ing-form*, then the *ing-form* of the verb has secondary stress. Practice the following.

1. start getting dinner
2. stopped reading the book
3. began buying clothes
4. likes playing the piano
5. delayed starting the game
6. wouldn't stop singing the song
7. didn't fear hearing the truth
8. can't delay starting the game
9. didn't enjoy hearing the lecture
10. doesn't like painting pictures

Practice Sentences

1. Mr. Johnson finished eating dinner.
2. Mary began playing the piano.
3. Dr. James started making his calls.
4. Mrs. Green enjoys cleaning the house.
5. Mr. Rice enjoys playing cards.
6. Betty doesn't like doing the dishes.
7. We didn't fear hearing the truth.
8. They couldn't delay starting the game.
9. She doesn't enjoy driving a car.
10. Henry wouldn't stop reading the book.

Adjectives

Two Adjectives in a series

If two adjectives precede a noun, they both have secondary stress.

1. • — — ′
a big black cat
a large white house
a long black car
the tall thin boy

2. • — • — ′
an angry young man
a pretty green ball
a funny old man
some dirty white shoes

3. • — • • — ′
a beautiful gold watch
a wonderful new car
an interesting old desk
a marvelous green desk

Practice Sentences

1. She wrote a long interesting letter.
2. The boy had a pretty orange balloon.
3. He gave her a large, expensive gift.
4. It was a big tall tree.
5. He's a tired hungry boy.
6. Jane bought a beautiful green dress.
7. He was a funny old man.
8. He was wearing some dirty white shoes.
9. It was a beautiful white bird.
10. They bought a charming old house.

Two Adjectives before a Noun Compound

1. pretty new sewing machine
2. seven bad traffic accidents
3. beautiful gold wristwatch
4. big red fire engine
5. long difficult grammar book
6. old established newspaper

7. big juicy pineapple
8. big black suitcase
9. white fluffy popcorn
10. interesting old teapot
11. eight new classrooms

Practice Sentences

1. He gave her a beautiful gold wristwatch.
2. The fire department bought a new red fire engine.
3. He was carrying a big black suitcase.
4. Our school has two new classrooms.
5. She showed us an interesting old teapot.
6. Mrs. Smith bought a pretty new sewing machine.
7. The children went to a large gay amusement park.
8. John has a new green fountain pen.
9. The Sentinel is an old established newspaper.
10. They delivered the shiny new farm equipment.

Noun Compounds—Longer Forms

In section three we studied noun compounds. Here are a few examples.

filling station	speech improvement
drugstore	air conditioning
airplane	department store
armchair	ping pong
football	roller skating
basketball	baseball

Compounds such as these may be combined with still another word to form a longer compound. These are also noun compounds. In these longer compounds, the stress pattern of the first two words is primary-tertiary. The loudest stress of the third word is secondary. Here are some examples:

filling station attendant	speech improvement class
drugstore clerk	air conditioning unit
airplane mechanic	department store manager
armchair cover	ping-pong table

football game   roller skating rink
basketball game   baseball bat

Practice Sentences

1   It was an exciting basketball game.
2. He's an excellent airplane mechanic.
3. Do you know the new filling station attendant?
4. We bought a new ping-pong table.
5. Their school has a large new basketball court
6. Our house has a new air conditioning unit.
7. Mr. Jones is the new department store manager.
8. I'm going to ask the drugstore clerk.
9. Our town has a new roller skating rink.
10. Bobby bought a new baseball bat.

Noun Compounds as Subjects

When a noun compound is the subject of the sentence, the primary stress of the first word of the compound is reduced to secondary stress.

Practice Sentences

1. Her sewing machine is new.
2. The basketball game was very exciting.
3. That baseball bat is too heavy.
4. The airplane mechanic is my friend.
5. The department store is on the next corner.
6. The filling station attendant was very helpful.
7. Our new air conditioning unit works fine.
8. The farm equipment was delivered yesterday.
9. The police department is in the next block.
10. Your armchair needs a new cover.

8. WORD COMBINATION STRESS (4) MINOR STRESS

Two-Word Verbs   *(Tape 10 begins here)*

The stress pattern of separable two-word verbs is tertiary-primary. The verb has tertiary stress; the adverb has primary stress.

1.   ⁻ ′   2.   ⁻ • ′   3.   ⁻ ′ •

put on   give away   do over
take off   put aside   look over
turn on   turn around   think over
turn off   put away   move over
wear out   ⁻ bring about   turn over

If there is a pronoun object, it always comes between the verb and adverb. The pronoun object always has weak stress.

4.   ⁻ • ′   5.   ⁻ • • ′   6.   ⁻ • ′ •

put it on   gave it away   did it over
take them off   put them aside   looked them over
turn it on   turn it around   thought it over
turn it off   put them away   move them over
wore them out   brought it about   turn it over

Practice Sentences

1. My shoes are very old. I've worn them out.
2. His homework was wrong. He had to do it over.
3. I don't know what to do. I'll have to think it over.
4. My car won't run. I'll have to fix it up.
5. The radio bothers me. Please turn it off.
6. Some of these coins may be valuable. I want to look them over.
7. The desk won't fit here. Let's turn it around.
8. My watch wouldn't work. I gave it away.

65

Two-Word Verbs with a noun object following

When a noun object follows the two-word verb, the noun receives the primary stress. The verb has tertiary stress, and the adverb, secondary stress.

Put on your shoes.   Put away your toys.
Take off your coat.   Do over the lesson.
Turn on the light.   Look over the letter.

Practice Sentences

1. He put on his shoes.
2. We took off our coats.
3. She turned on the light.
4. He gave away his toys.
5. He hung up his coat.

6. She put away her clothes.
7. The immigration man looked over our papers.
8. I have to put away the car.
9. The Smiths fixed up their house.
10. I picked out a nice gift.

Two-word verbs with a noun object between

When a two-word verb is separated by a noun object, the noun usually receives the primary stress.

tried the coat on   put his clothes away
gave his toys away   looked the information up
called his friend up

Practice Sentences

1. I put my coat on.
2. I asked him to take his hat off.
3. She couldn't turn the switch on.
4. I've worn my suit out.
5. Please turn the radio off.

6. She tried the dress on.
7. I want to call my friend up.
8. Please put your coat away.
9. I picked a gift out.
10. We fixed the house up.

Object Pronouns

Object pronouns are spoken with either tertiary stress or weak stress. In rapid speech, when the reduced forms are generally used ('er for *her*, 'im for *him*, ya for *you*, 'em for *them*) they have weak stress. If the speech is a little slower and more deliberate, they will likely have the full form (*him, her, you, them*) with tertiary stress.

1. ´ –
see you
hear him
call her
ask them
help me

2. — ´ –
can't hear them
won't help her
don't tell us

3. — · ´ –
didn't call us
wouldn't tell him
couldn't help her

4. — · ´ · – –
didn't recognize us

5. — · – · ´ –
didn't understand him

6. — · · ´ –
wouldn't permit us

7. — – · ´ –
can't recommend him

8. — · ´ · –
don't remember them

9. — · ´ · – –
didn't telephone me

Practice Sentences

1. Please hélp mē.
2. Wē dīdn't sée hēr.
3. Dīd yōu téll hīm?
4. Wē dīdn't ásk them.
5. Thēy dīdn't récognīze ūs.

6. Dīdn't thēy téll yōu?
7. Īt dīdn't húrt mē.
8. Dīd yōu wríte hēr?
9. Plēase dón't bóther mē.
10. Whȳ dón't yōu cáll them?

Listen to these sentences. The object pronouns are spoken with weak stress.

1. Dōn't téll him.
2. Wē dīdn't sée hēr.
3. Dō you knów him?
4. Wē dīdn't ásk them.
5. Thēy dīdn't récognīze us.

6. Dīdn't thēy téll yōu?
7. Whāt dīd yōu téll hēr?
8. Dīd yōu wríte hēr?
9. Hē hāsn't cálled us.
10. Ī cān't fínd them.

Object Pronouns—following verb and preposition

In this case the pronoun almost always has weak stress. The preposition will usually have tertiary stress.

1. ´ – ·
do with it
go with us
read to them
speak to us

2. ´ · – ·
know about it
tell about it
write about him
speak about it

Practice Sentences

1. Whāt dīd yōu dó wīth it?
2. Cān yōu gó wīth us?
3. Bōbby's mōther réads tō him.
4. Thēy dīdn't spéak tō us.
5. Whāt dīd yōu wríte ābōut him?

6. Ī dōn't līke tō tálk ābōut it.
7. Dīd Hēnry knów ābōut it?
8. Ī wānt yōu tō lísten tō mē.
9. Ī hōpe yōu'll wríte tō us.
10. Whāt dīd shē sáy ābōut it?

Two Object Pronouns following a verb

Both pronoun objects usually have weak stress. In more deliberate speech, the second object pronoun may have tertiary stress.

give it to me
sell it to him
write him for me
help me with it
read it to her
do it for them
buy them for her
send it to us

Practice Sentences

1. I want you to give it to me.
2. Won't you sell it to him?
3. Will you write him for me?
4. I hope you can help me with it.

5. Her mother read it to her.
6. Will you do it for them?
7. I told Mary I'd buy it for her.
8. I'd like you to send it to us.

Object Pronouns—After noun and a preposition

The object pronoun has weak stress in rapid speech; it has tertiary stress in deliberate speech. These differences in stress are very slight. The important thing to remember is to say object pronouns with a minor stress (tertiary or weak).

Practice Sentences

1. Please open the window for me.
2. The rug has a spot on it.
3. Will you do a favor for me?
4. My car has a heater in it.

5. This safe doesn't have a lock on it.
6. Mary showed her new dress to us.
7. He put a piece of wood under it.

Object Pronouns—After adjective and a preposition

Again the object pronoun may have tertiary or weak stress depending on the rate of speech.

slow	*rapid*	*slow*	*rapid*
good for you	good for you	honest about it	honest about it
happy for them	happy for them	glad for you	glad for you
useful to me	useful to me	good on her	good on her
nice of her	nice of her		

Practice Sentences

1. T̄ake th̄is médicine.   It's góod for̄ yo͞u.
2. J̄une is ḡetting márried.   I'm ver̄y háppẏ for̄ her̈.
3. Th̄ank yo͞u for̄ the̊ knife.   It'll b̄e ver̄y úsefu̇l to͞ me̅.
4. I'm gl̄ad M̄arthå hélped yo͞u. Th̄at was ver̄y niće o͞f her̈.
5. Ī kno͞w h̄e d̄id wróng.   But I'm gl̄ad h̄e was hónest ȧbo͞ut it.
6. Sh̄e ḡot the̊ lēad īn the̊ pláy   I'm glád for̄ her̈.
7. M̄arẏ bóught å n̄ew dréss.   Īt lo͞oks ver̄y góod ōn her̈.

Verbs

Verbs followed by *to* and the base form of another verb

Certain verbs can be followed by the word *to* and the base form of another verb, (*want to go, like to win*). In this case the word *to* always has weak stress. The verb used with *to* usually has tertiary stress.

These verbs can also be used with the word *to* without the following base form of another verb (*I want to, I'd like to*). When they are used in this manner, the word *to* often has tertiary stress.

1. ⁻ ˙ ′   2. ′ ⁻   3. ⁻ ˙ ′ ⁻

want to go	want to	doesn't want to
like to come	like to	didn't like to
used to drive	used to	didn't used to
have to work	have to	don't have to
hope to win	hope to	didn't hope to
ought to go	ought to	

Practice Sentences

1. D̄o yo͞u w̄ant to̊ gó?   Yés. Ī wánt to̅.
2. W̄ould yo͞u līke to̊ cóme?   Yés. I'd líke to̅.
3. D̄id yo͞u ūse to̊ drив́e?   Yés. Ī úsed to̅.
4. D̄oes h̄e h̄ave to̊ wórk?   Yés. H̄e hás to̅.
5. D̄id th̄ey hōpe to̊ wiń?   Yés. Th̄ey hóped to̅.
6. Āre yo͞u gōing to̊ trý?   Yés. I'm góing̊ to̅.
7. D̄on't yo͞u w̄ant to̊ gó?   Nó. Ī d̄on't wánt to̅.
8. D̄oesn't h̄e h̄ave to̊ wórk?   Nó. H̄e d̄oesn't háve to̅.
9. Āre yo͞u gōing to̊ cóme?   Nó. I'm n̄ot góing to̅.
10. Āren't yo͞u su̇ppōsed to̊ wáit? Nó. I'm n̄ot su̇ppósed to̅.

Question Words

Question words (*who, what, when, where, which, why, how*) may have tertiary stress in certain situations.

When question words are used in indirect questions, they usually have tertiary stress. Listen to the following examples:

Ī dōn't knōw whō hē iś.   Dō you knōw whȳ hē is cóming?

Dō you knōw whāt īt iś?   Dīd shē sāy whēn shē wȧs léaving?

Ī dōn't knōw hōw tȯ dó ı̇t.   Ī dōn't knōw whēre īt iś.

When the question words *how, what, which* are used before another word to form a question phrase, they usually have tertiary stress.

Hōw lōng ı̇s thė táblė?   Whīch magȧzīne ı̇s yóurs?

Hōw fār is īt tȯ thė nēxt tówn?   Whīch ōne dīd you wȧnt?

Whāt bōok ȧre you réadı̇ng?   Hōw manẏ dō you háve?

Whāt tīme ı̇s hė léavı̇ng?

one and *ones* — Following Adjectives

When the words *one* or *ones* follow adjectives, they always have weak stress.

1. ´ ·	2. ´ · ·	3. · ´ · ·
good one	pretty one	important one
nice one	yellow one	attractive one
long one	orange one	convenient one
black one	modern one	exciting one
big one	happy one	amusing one
that one	biggest one	delightful one
this one	smallest one	another one

Practice Sentences

1. Dō you wānt thė yéllȯw ȯne?   3. Wōuld you tāke thė smállėst ȯne?
2. Dīd hė līke thė módėrn ȯne?   4. Dīd shē buy thė préttẏ ȯne?

Practice Questions and Answers

1. Whīch ōne dō you wȧnt?   Ī wānt thė bést ȯne.
2. Dīd hė buȳ ȧ cár?   Yés. Hē bōught ȧ bláck ȯne.
3. Dīd you līke thė móvı̇e?   Yés. It wȧs ȧ góod ȯne.
4. Whīch ōne dīd you buy?   Ī bōught thė expénsı̇ve ȯne.
5. Āre you gōing tȯ thė méetı̇ng?   Yés. It's ȧ vēry impórtȧnt ȯne.
6. Īs thȧt ȧ gōod bóok?   Yés. It's ȧ vēry ȧmúsı̇ng ȯne.

The Word — *than* — in Comparative Sentences

The word *than* may have either weak or tertiary stress when it is used in comparative sentences. If it has tertiary stress, it is pronounced /ðæn/; if it has weak stress, it is pronounced /ðən/. It is usually pronounced with weak stress.

Practice Sentences

1. Planes are faster than cars.
2. John is taller than Bill.
3. June is shorter than Joyce.
4. Milk is better than tea.
5. This is better than that.

6. This one is better than that one.
7. These are more expensive than those.
8. Mr. Smith is more interesting than his wife.
9. The book was more exciting than the movie.
10. Japanese is more difficult than English.

as . . . as — in Comparative Sentences

When the word *as* is used in comparative sentences, it has weak stress and is pronounced /əz/.

Practice Sentences

1. Orlon is as warm as wool.
2. That plane is as fast as sound.
3. That star is as bright as a diamond.
4. My feet are as cold as ice.
5. She is as pretty as a picture.
6. He's as mean as a bear.
7. You're as sound as a dollar.
8. She's as happy as a lark.
9. He's as quiet as a mouse.
10. He's as sly as a fox.

11. It was as slippery as an eel.
12. It was as straight as an arrow.
13. It's as light as a feather.
14. It's as easy as pie.
15. It was as clean as a whistle.
16. His face was as red as a beet.
17. It was as green as grass.
18. He was as white as a ghost.
19. It's as heavy as lead.
20. You're as right as rain.

9. INTONATION (2)

Tag Questions *(Tape 11 begins here)*

Three different intonations can be used with sentences with tag questions with slight differences in meaning. Two types are given in this section; the third type is illustrated in *Stress and Intonation, Part 2*, Section 8. Type 1 is the most common.

Type 1 /232:2 ⤴/

Yōu cȧn dó ȧt, cán't yōu?	Yēs, Ī cán.
He is coming, isn't he?	Yes, he is.
You were trying, weren't you?	Yes, I was.

The same intonation is used for the negative form.

Hē wōn't dó ȧt, wíll hē?	Nō, hē wón't.
She can't see it, can she?	No, she can't.
They weren't trying, were they?	No, they weren't.

Practice Sentences

1. Rūth īsn't góȧng, ȧs shē?
2. Dr. Nēlsȯn dīdn't cáll, dȧd hē?
3. Wē āren't láte, áre wē?
4. Jōhn hāsn't cóme, hás hē?
5. Mȑs. Whīte ȧccepted thē īnvitátion, dȧdn't shē?

72

6. Yōu càn hēar thè spéakèr, cán't yōu?

7. Yōu hāven't sēen mỳ fóuntàin pēn, háve yōu?

8. Thē rādiò's tūrned ón, isn't īt?

9. Yōu wānt thè bíggèst òne, dón't yōu?

10. Mrs. Nēlsòn wāsn't ángrỳ, wás shē?

11. Mr. Pāttersòn wōuld līke tò cóme, wóuldn't hē?

12. Īt dīdn't húrt, did ìt?

13. Thāt's à nēw básebāll bāt, isn't īt?

14. Yōu līke plāyìng thè piáno, dón't yōu?

15. Īt's rāthèr lóng, isn't it?

Special note

As was pointed out, the declarative intonation pattern steps down (⌐L) from pitch 3 to a lower pitch if one or more syllables follow the one with primary stress in the phrase; it glides down (⌐\) if the stressed syllable is final in the phrase. In this book, either pattern will be taken to mean one or the other, and the appearance of the step or the glide pattern at the head of an exercise will not indicate that all the sentences in the drill necessarily match the example in this respect. The student should automatically select the step or the glide pattern according to the position of the stressed syllable in the phrase.

Type 1 with Direct Address /232·2·2 ⤴/

A tag question can be directed to someone by name. In this case, the intonation is as shown.

You càn dó ìt,   càn't yōu, Bíll?
You remémber,   don't you, Ruth?
You're forgetting, aren't you, Don?

Practice Sentences

1. Yōu càn cóme, cán't yōu, Mrs. Cháse?

2. Yōur hūsbànd remémbèrs mē, dóesn't hē, Hélèn?

3. Yōu've séen ìt, háven't yōu, Bób?

4. Yōu're gōìng tò réad ìt, áren't yōu, Jéff?

5. Yōu'd līke tò gó, wóuldn't yōu, Mrs. Hóuse?

6. Yōur hūsbànd's à láwyèr, isn't hē, Mrs. Gílpìn?

7. Yōu hāven't mēt Dr. Wílsòn, háve yōu, Júne?

8. Yōu dīdn't fāil thè exám, did yōu, Rúth?

9. Yōu aren't léaving, áre yōu, Mrs. Jámes?
10. You've quīt smóking, háven't yōu, Mr. White?

Type 2 /231 31/

When you use this intonation, you are probably a little more sure that you are going to get the confirmation you expect.

You knōw her, dón't yōu?   Yes, Ī dó.
You've seen him, haven't you?   Yes, I have.
You'll tell him, won't him?   Yes, I will.

Practice Sentences

1. The gāme was excíting, wásn't it?   6. This is a gōod réstaurant, ísn't it?
2. Yōu were thére, wéren't yōu?   7. Yōu can't dó it, cán yōu?
3. This is the préttiest óne, ísn't it?   8. Yōu were wróng about it, wéren't yōu?
4. Yōu dīdn't fíx it, díd yōu?   9. She dīdn't spéak to yōu, díd she?
5. The plāy was amúsing, wásn't it?   10. Wē shōuld téll hīm, shóuldn't wē?

Type 2 with Direct Address /231 31 1/

When a Type 2 tag question is directed to someone by name, the name is usually said on the pitch 1 level without a rise.

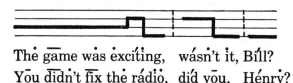

The gāme was excíting,   wásn't it, Bíll?
Yōu dīdn't fīx the rádio,   díd yōu,   Hénry?

Practice Sentences

1. The plāy was amúsing, wásn't it, Hélen?
2. Mrs. Smīth wasn't vēry níce to us, wás she, Rúth?
3. Yōu tōld Máry, dídn't yōu, Jóhn?
4. Yōu dīdn't dō your hómework, díd yōu, Jóhnny?
5. This steāk īsn't vēry góod, ís it, Émily?

Clauses—/231/

When a clause beginning with a connecting word (*before*, *when*, *since*, *because*, *if*, etc.) comes as the second part of a sentence, the sentence is often said as one phrase with one primary stress.

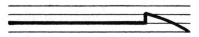

I'll tell him when he cómes.
We went to bed after they léft.
They did it because they hád to.

Clauses—/232 231/

Sentences with clauses are more commonly said in two phrases. The longer the sentence, the more likely there will be two phrases in the sentence.

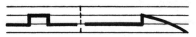

I'll téll him when he cómes.
We went to béd after they léft.
They díd it because they hád to.

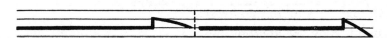

I had finished all my wórk before the clock struck tén.
Mr. and Mrs. Johnson arríved before we were ready to gó.

Practice Sentences

Practice these sentences using two phrases.

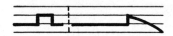

1. I'll dó it if I have tíme.
2. We changed our clóthes before we ate dínner.
3. I want to see the móvie because I've heard it's very góod.
4. He had never seen a fóotball game until he went to New Yórk.
5. The children came in the hóuse after they finished pláying.
6. The game was óver when I arríved.
7. You'd better wear glóves when you go skíing.
8. Mrs. Jones listens to the rádio while she gets dínner.

9. Hē laughed ōut lóud¦whīle hė wàs réading.
10. Marẏ can't stānd nóise¦whīle shē stúdies.

Clauses — /232 ⌐ ¦231/

When a clause comes as the first element in a sentence, there is usually a slight rise at the end of the first phrase.

Befōre hē wént,   hē cālled hīs óffice.
Āftėr hē cómes, lēt's gō dōwntówn.
Whēn yōu sée hėr, tēll hėr Ī cálled.
Īf Ī hād mónėy, Ī'd trável.

Practice Sentences

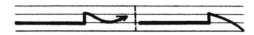

1. Āftėr thėy dánced, thēy wėre tíred.
2. Befōre Ī réalīzed ìt, shē wàs góne.
3. Ūntīl ìt ráins, īt wīll bē dústẏ.
4. Becāuse hē hād clássės, hē couldn't gō àwáy.
5. Sīnce ìt wàs wōrn óut, thēy gòt anóthėr óne.
6. Īf yōu're gōing tò dó ìt, dō ìt nów.
7. Whēn thė līght tūrned gréen, thēy crōssed thė stréet.
8. Whīle hė stúdied, nō òne tálked.
9. Āftėr hē sáid ìt, hė smiĺed.
10. Whēn thė tēlephōne ráng, wē wėre ēating dínnėr.

Counting

There are several different intonations that can be used when counting.

(1) /31 31 31/

This is a slow, deliberate way of counting. The voice begins on pitch level 3, and drops to pitch 1. The voice stops, and then the next number is given in the same way.

ōne   twō   thrée   fóur   fíve   síx   sévėn   eíght

(2) /3 3 31/

This is a more rapid way of counting. In this case all the numbers are said on the pitch 3 level until the last one, which begins on pitch 3 and drops to pitch 1. The /31/ intonation at the end signals that the speaker has finished counting.

Note that the *teen* numbers, *thirteen, fourteen,* etc., have the primary stress on the first syllable when counting.

twénty	thírty	fórty	fífty	síxty
síxteen	séventeen	éighteen	níneteen	twénty
thrée	fóur	fíve	síx	séven
twélve	thírteen	fóurteen	fífteen	síxteen

(3) /2 2 3 1/

This is a more common way of counting. The voice remains on the pitch 2 level until the last number which is spoken with a /31/ intonation. The /31/ intonation at the end indicates that the speaker has finished counting.

óne	twó	thrée	fóur	fíve
éight	níne	tén	eléven	twélve
fíve	síx	séven	éight	níne
fífty	síxty	séventy	éighty	nínety

If one or more syllables precede the syllable with primary stress, then the intonation of the last number is /231/.

/2 2 231/

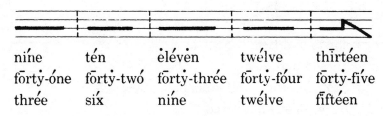

níne	tén	eléven	twélve	thírteen
fórty-óne	fórty-twó	fórty-thrée	fórty-fóur	fórty-fíve
thrée	síx	níne	twélve	fífteen

(4) /2 ⤴ 2 ⤴ (2)31 /

It is also very common to count on the pitch 2 level, using a rising voice after each number except the last one. The intonation of the last number is either / 31/ (on such numbers as *ten, sixty, twelve*) or /231/ on such numbers as *twenty-five, fifteen,* which have syllables preceding the primary stress.

six   séven   éight níne tén
twénty   thírty   fórty   fífty síxty
fóur   síx   éight tén   twélve

fíve   tén   fífteen   twénty   twenty-fíve
thrée   síx   níne   twélve   fiftéen
twenty-séven twenty-éight twenty-níne thírty   thirty-óne

Listing /2 ⌐ |2 ⌐ |231/

This intonation is used when listing several items in an affirmative or negative statement.

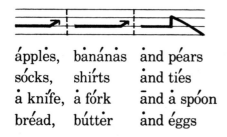

ápples,   banánas and péars
sócks,   shírts   and tíes
a knífe,   a fórk   and a spóon
bréad,   bútter   and éggs

Practice Sentences

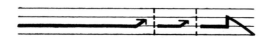

1. Í bought some sócks, shírts and tíes.
2. Pléase get some mílk, bréad and méat.
3. We have órange júice, tomáto júice, and píneapple júice.
4. The líttle bóy was húngry, sléepy and tíred.
5. Í got my cár óiled, gréased and repáired.
6. I'd líke some bácon, éggs and tóast.
7. She has a lót of drésses, shóes and háts.
8. I'd líke some céreal, cóffee and júice.
9. Í don't líke ráin, snów or sléet.
10. All he dóes is sléep, éat and pláy.

Common Phrases /2⌐/

A very few common words and phrases are spoken on the 2 level with a slight rise.

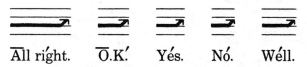

All right.   O.K.   Yés.   Nó.   Wéll.

Questions

Limited Choice—/23⁝231/ or /23 ⌐⁝231/

This type of question is used when a person is asked to choose between alternatives and the choice is limited.

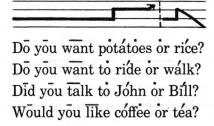

Dō you wānt potátoes or ríce?
Dō you wānt to ríde or wálk?
Dīd you tālk to Jóhn or Bíll?
Wōuld you līke cóffee or téa?

Practice Sentences

1. Wōuld you līke cóffee⁝or mílk?
2. Dō you wānt a sháve⁝or a háircūt?
3. Īs it súnny⁝or clóudy?
4. Dīd you stāy hóme⁝or gō óut?
5. Wōuld you līke péas⁝or cárrots?
6. Wās shē háppy⁝or sád?
7. Īs the trāffic līght gréen⁝or réd?
8. Wōuld you līke some frúit⁝or some cándy?
9. Dīd you sée her⁝or tálk to her?
10. Dō you prefēr wātching télevīsion⁝or gōing to the móvies?

There may be, of course, a choice between three or more alternatives. In this case the intonation is either /23 ⌐ ⁝3⁝231/ or /23 ⌐ ⁝23 ⌐ ⁝231/.

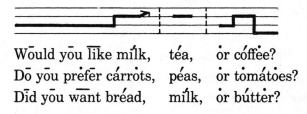

Wōuld you līke mílk,   téa,   or cóffee?
Dō you prefēr cárrots,   péas,   or tomátoes?
Dīd you wānt bréad,   mílk,   or bútter?

The intonation of the second phrase may be /23 ↗/ if there are one or more syllables which precede the syllable with primary stress.

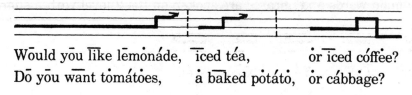

Would you līke lēmonáde,   īced téa,   or īced cóffee?
Do you wānt tomátoes,   a bāked potáto, or cábbage?

Practice Sentences

1. Does shē pīay thē piáno, the hárp, or the violín?
2. Would you līke wáter, milk, or cóffee?
3. Does hē līve īn New Yórk, Chicágo, or Dénver?
4. Shāll wē gō for a drive, take a wálk, or stāy at hóme?
5. Wās thāt her móther, her sister, or a cóusin?
6. Do you wānt to gō nów, láter, or nōt āt áll?
7. Do you wānt to rēad a bóok, watch télevision, or gō tō a móvie?

Unlimited Choice — /23 23 23 ↗ / or /23 ↗ 23 ↗ 23 ↗/

This type of intonation is used when choices are offered, but they are not restricted. That is, there may be still other choices that can be made and the speaker is not limiting the choices to the ones he has mentioned.

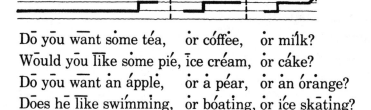

Do you wānt some téa,   or cóffee, or milk?
Would you līke some pié, ice cream, or cáke?
Do you wānt an ápple,   or a péar, or an órange?
Does hē līke swímming, or bóating, or íce skāting?

Practice Sentences

1. Do you līke músic, or árt, or the dráma?
2. Do you nēed āny shirts, or sócks, or tíes?
3. Does shē nēed āny shóes, or stóckings, or swéaters?
4. Do you thīnk īt's gōing to ráin, or snów, or sléet?
5. Do you wānt to stāy hóme, or gō óut, or rēad a gōod bóok?
6. Would you līke órange jūice, tomáto jūice, or píneapple jūice?
7. Would you līke some céreal, or éggs, or tóast?
8. Does hē līke básketbāll, or fóotbāll, or báisebāll?

Calling—/32/

This type of intonation is used when calling to someone, usually at some distance away. A mother calling her child outdoors would use this intonation.

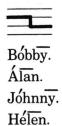

Bóbby.
Álan.
Jóhnny.
Hélen.
Bétty.

Warning or Cautioning—/23/

You will hear this intonation when someone is cautioning or reprimanding. If a child is doing something he shouldn't, or is about to do something, you will hear the parent say his name in the following manner:

Jóhnny.
Bóbby.
Álan.
Bétty.
Génevieve.

Practice Dialog 1

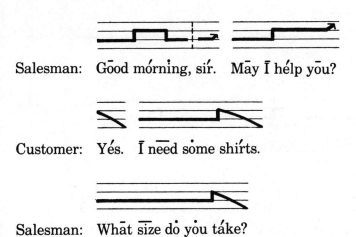

Salesman: Good mórning, sír. Máy I hélp you?

Customer: Yés. I need some shírts.

Salesman: Whát size do you táke?

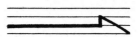

Customer: Fīftēen-thīrtȳ-fóur.

Salesman: Anȳ pártīcūlár cólor?

Customer: Yés.   Ī wānt ōne whíte shīrt ānd ōne blúe óne.

Salesman: Hére wē āre, sír.   Thēse sēll fōr fīve-fīftȳ ápiéce.

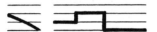

Customer: Fíne.   Ī'll táke thėm.

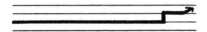

Salesman: Wīll thėre bē ānȳthing élse?

Dō yȯu nēed sócks, ȯr tiés, ȯr hándkėrchiefs?

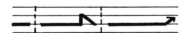

Customer: Nó, nōt tȯdáy, thánk yōu.

Salesman: Āll ríght.   Thāt wīll bē ėlēvėn dóllȧrs fȯr thė twō shírts, sír.

Customer: Hére yōu āre.

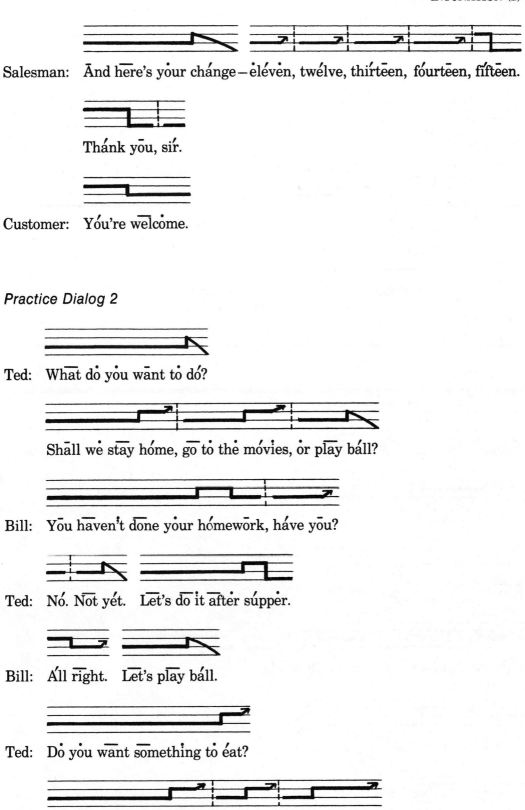

Salesman: And here's your change — eleven, twelve, thirteen, fourteen, fifteen.

Thank you, sir.

Customer: You're welcome.

Practice Dialog 2

Ted: What do you want to do?

Shall we stay home, go to the movies, or play ball?

Bill: You haven't done your homework, have you?

Ted: No. Not yet. Let's do it after supper.

Bill: All right. Let's play ball.

Ted: Do you want something to eat?

Would you like an apple, or a pear, or a banana?

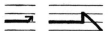

Bill: I'll take an ápple.

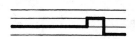

Ted: O.K.' Let's gó.

Bill: That's a new báseball bat, isn't it?

Ted: Yés. I got it yésterday.

Bill: Swéll.

Ted: Did you see the báseball game Sunday?

Bill: Yés. It was exciting, wásn't it?

Ted: It sure wás. I'm glad we wón.

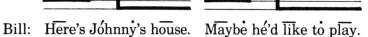

Bill: Here's Jóhnny's house. Maybe he'd like to play.

Ted: All right. Cáll him.

Bill: Jóhnny. Jóhnny.

10. NUMBERS AND DATES—STRESS WITH AFFIXES—RHYTHM

Numbers and Dates   *(Tape 12 begins here)*

Numbers

When spoken aloud, numbers are divided into phrases according to millions, thousands, and hundreds.

When reading numbers in the hundreds, the word *and* is used after the word *hundred* by some speakers, but not by others.

102	one hundred two	one hundred and two
624	six hundred twenty-four	six hundred and twenty-four
341	three hundred forty-one	three hundred and forty-one
555	five hundred fifty-five	five hundred and fifty-five
864	eight hundred sixty-four	eight hundred and sixty-four

Numbers in the thousands are usually spoken in two phrases.

5,298	five thousand,	two hundred ninety-eight
6,452	six thousand,	four hundred fifty-two
4,984	four thousand,	nine hundred eighty-four
1,111	one thousand,	one hundred and eleven
6,765	six thousand,	seven hundred sixty-five
51,929	fifty-one thousand,	nine hundred twenty-nine
68,109	sixty-eight thousand,	one hundred and nine
42,477	forty-two thousand,	four hundred seventy-seven
22,222	twenty-two thousand,	two hundred and twenty-two
33,333	thirty-three thousand,	three hundred and thirty-three

348,999   three hundred forty-eight thousand, nine hundred ninety-nine
666,666   six hundred sixty-six thousand,   six hundred and sixty-six
456,789   four hundred fifty-six thousand,   seven hundred eighty-nine
222,222   two hundred twenty-two thousand, two hundred twenty-two
333,333   three hundred thirty-three thousand, three hundred and thirty-three

1,416,921   one million,   four hundred sixteen thousand, nine hundred twenty-one
4,512,846   four million, five hundred twelve thousand,   eight hundred forty-six
5,555,555   five million, five hundred fifty-five thousand, five hundred fifty-five
1,202,568   one million,   two hundred and two thousand, five hundred sixty-eight
40,102,621   forty million, one hundred and two thousand, six hundred and twenty-one

Practice reading these numbers:

616	429	777	492	999
5,412	4,111	6,666	12,419	50,421
512,919	444,444	333,333	123,456	912,619
1,666,798	4,222,345	3,333,333	51,622,547	100,643,231

Fractions

Fractions of the following types are read with the word *and*. Practice the following examples.

14½   fourteen and a half
14¾   fourteen and three-fourths (*or*) fourteen and three quarters
16¼   sixteen and one-fourth (*or*) sixteen and a quarter
17⅜   seventeen and three-eighths
19 4/9   nineteen and four-ninths
12⅕   twelve and one-fifth (*or*) twelve and a fifth
48 3/16   forty-eight and three-sixteenths

Fractions written with decimal points may be read in more than one way. Use of the word *point* is more common in technical style and for long fractions. Listen to the following examples:

14.5   fourteen and a half
        fourteen and five-tenths
        fourteen point five

16.78   sixteen and seventy-eight hundredths
        sixteen point seven eight

4.916   four and nine hundred sixteen thousandths
        four point nine one six

29.1   twenty-nine and one-tenth
            twenty-nine point one

6.91762   six point nine one seven six two

Read the following, using the word *and*:

$14\frac{1}{2}$	fourteen and a half	$21\frac{3}{8}$
$14\frac{3}{4}$		$12\frac{4}{9}$
$19\frac{9}{10}$		$42\frac{3}{16}$

Read the following, using the word *and*:

1.7	one and seven tenths	1.02	one and two hundredths
6.2		4.03	
4.3		6.99	
5.8		5.45	
9.9		3.33	

Read the following, using the word *point*:

7.1	seven point one	21.798
12.2		16.64592
16.4		12.23456789
19.68		

Dates

There are four different elements that can be used when giving the time and date. They are:

Time	Day of Week	Month and Day	Year and Era
4:30 a.m.	Monday	January 15	1966 A.D.

When saying dates, each of the above elements is usually said in a phrase. If two of the categories are present, there are two phrases; if there are three elements, then there are three phrases, etc. Listen to the following:

one phrase

4:30	four thirty
5:30 a.m.	five thirty a.m.
Monday	Monday
January	January
January 15	January fifteenth
April 21	April twenty first
1966 A.D.	nineteen sixty-six A.D.
2000 B.C.	two thousand B.C.

two phrases

four thirty-five a.m.,   Mónday
six forty-eight p.m.,   Thursday
nine twenty-five a.m., Saturday

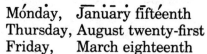

Mónday,   Jánuary fiftéenth
Thursday, August twenty-first
Friday,   March eighteenth

Jánuary,   nineteen sixty-six
August,   seventeen seventy-seven
February, eighteen forty-eight

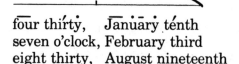

four thirty,   Jánuary ténth
seven o'clock, February third
eight thirty,   August nineteenth

three phrases

Mónday,   Jánuary fiftéenth,   nineteen sixty-six
Tuesday,   August nineteenth, eighteen forty-nine
Thursday, July twenty-first,   sixteen forty-two

four thirty p.m., Mónday,   Jánuary fiftéenth
seven o'clock,   Thursday, February twenty-first
six thirty p.m., Friday,   July twenty-eighth

The time and the day may be said in one phrase.

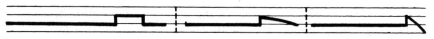

four thirty a.m., Mónday,   Jánuary fiftéenth, nineteen sixty-six
seven o'clock,   Thursday, February ninth,   eighteen ninety-two
six thirty p.m., Saturday, August twelfth,   fourteen thirty-two

Practice reading the following dates:

1. June 10, 1979
    April 21, 1616
    June 19, 1499
    August 12, 1313
    December 20, 1980

2. Monday, January 16
    Saturday, February 12
    Sunday, March 16
    Thursday, November 28
    Friday, April 5

3. 4:30 p.m., Monday
    6:35 p.m., Tuesday
    12:00 noon, Saturday
    4:00 a.m., Sunday
    7:35 p.m., Wednesday

4. Monday, August 16, 1778
    Wednesday, September 14, 1999
    Thursday, July 4, 1776
    Friday, November 25, 1478
    Tuesday, October 9, 1521

Telephone numbers

In the United States, telephone numbers usually consist of seven numbers. The first three numbers are read in one phrase, the following four numbers are read in a second phrase. Listen to the following:

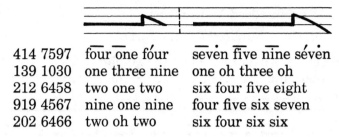

414 7597	four one four	seven five nine seven
139 1030	one three nine	one oh three oh
212 6458	two one two	six four five eight
919 4567	nine one nine	four five six seven
202 6466	two oh two	six four six six

If you are calling long distance, there is an area code consisting of three numbers which precedes the telephone number. These are spoken in a phrase.

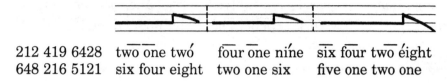

| 212 419 6428 | two one two | four one nine | six four two eight |
| 648 216 5121 | six four eight | two one six | five one two one |

Money

Usually the word *and* is used between the dollars and cents. If the units are clear from the context, the words *dollars* and *cents* may be omitted.

$4.26   four dollars and twenty-six cents
         four twenty-six

$426.00 four hundred twenty-six dollars
         four twenty-six

$301.01 three hundred and one dollars and one cent

$1,230.65 one thousand, two hundred thirty dollars and sixty-five cents

Addresses

In the United States, an address most commonly consists of (1) a number, (2) the name of a street or avenue, (3) city, (4) state.

If the words *avenue, lane,* or *road* are used, they generally have the phrase stress:

314 Maple Avenue	three fourteen Maple Avenue
1600 Pennsylvania Avenue	sixteen hundred Pennsylvania Avenue
919 Riggs Road	nine nineteen Riggs Road
1400 Cherry Lane	fourteen hundred Cherry Lane

If the word *street* is part of the address, however, the word preceding street generally has the phrase stress.

5210 Carlton Street   fifty-two ten Cárlton Street

1919 16th St.   nineteen nineteen Sixteenth Street

800 Main St.   eight hundred Máin Street

1400 Cherry Street   fourteen hundred Chérry Street

If the complete address is given, it is usually spoken in two phrases. The first phrase consists of the number and street, and the second contains the city and state. Listen to the following:

315 Maple Avenue, Atlanta, Georgia   three fifteen Maple Avenue, Atlanta, Géorgia

612 Cherry Lane, Denver, Colorado   six twelve Cherry Láne, Denver, Colorádo

2112 Ross Street, Buffalo, New York   twenty-one twelve Róss Street, Buffalo, New York

Practice Sentences

1.   He was born in 1919.
2.   He lives at 616 Summer Lane.
3.   I live at 1214 Main Street.
4.   It happened on Monday, January 19, 1816.
5.   The price is $3.99.
6.   His address is 115 Tulip Avenue, Miami, Florida.
7.   Her telephone number is 654 9211.
8.   I saw him on Thursday, August 22.
9.   It cost $316.25.
10. You can write to her at 666 Carlton Lane, Atlanta, Georgia.

Read these numbers and fractions

1.	616	4.	14½	7.	4,195
2.	5,280	5.	16.319	8.	409
3.	1,416,918	6.	66,666,666	9.	2,128
				10.	33,333

Words with Prefixes and Suffixes   *(Tape 13 begins here)*

When prefixes and suffixes are added to words in English, the position of the primary word stress often remains unchanged.

Prefix—with tertiary stress

anti-   sócial   antisócial

bi-   ánnual   biánnual

dis-	appróve	dìsappróve
ex-	président	ēx-président
non-	viólence	nōn-viólence
out-	wéigh	ōutwéigh
over-	éstimāte	ōveréstimāte
pan-	Américàn	Pān-Américàn
re-	dó	rēdó
sub-	maríne	sūbmaríne
trans-	cōntinéntàl	trānscōntinéntàl

Suffix — with weak stress

-able	sále	sáleablè
-al	cómìc	cómicàl
-en	Áfricà	Áfricàn
-ful	cáre	cáreful
-ish	sélf	sélfìsh
-less	cáre	cárelèss
-ly	lívè	lívelỳ
-ous	váry	várioùs
-y	lúck	lúckỳ

The prefix *re-*

The prefix *re-* when it means *again* is spoken with tertiary stress. Listen to the following examples:

rēmáke	rē-náme	rē-sórt	rē-láy
rēdó	rē-márk	rē-préss	rē-dréss

There are many words in English which begin with the letters *re*, but the *re* does not mean *again* and it is spoken with weak stress. Listen to these examples:

remárk	représs	redréss	resórt
refúse	reláy	redéem	redúce
			remínd

Here are a few pairs of words. The first column consists of words with *re-* prefix. The second column consists of words beginning with *re* spoken with weak stress.

re-prefix

rē-márk	remárk
rē-préss	représs
rē-láy	reláy
rē-dréss	redréss
rē-sórt	resórt

There are a few other prefixes which are spoken with tertiary stress—*de-, from;* *pre-, before; pro-, for.* Again there are other words which begin with the same letters and which are spoken with weak stress. Listen to the following examples.

Prefix *de-, from*

dērái̇l	dēríde
dēcȯmpóse	dēcli̇́ne

Prefix *pre-, before*

prē-pái̇d	prėpáred
prējúdge	prėténd
prēdáte	prėdi̇́ct

Prefix *pro-, for*

prō-lábȯr	prȯli̇́fic
prō-Frénch	prȯfáne
prō-Jāpȧnése	prȯjéct

Practice Sentences

1. When you redo this map, reduce the scale.
2. Remind me to remake the pocket of this dress.
3. He was a prolific writer of pro-labor pamphlets.
4. I predict that Arnold's discovery will pre-date yours.

The primary stress of a word sometimes shifts by the addition of a suffix. Listen to the following examples:

únivērse	ūnivérsȧl
tri̇́angle	tri̇́ángulȧr
sémici̇rcle	sēmici̇́rculȧr
mónosȳllȧble	mōnosȳllábic
múltiplȳ	mūltiplicátion
súbjėct	sūbjéctive
ádvērb	ādvérbiȧl

When the suffixes below are added to words, the primary stress of the word often shifts. There may also be vowel and final consonant changes.

Suffix

-ity	áctive (*adj.*)	actívity (*n.*)
-ify	sólid (*n.*)	solídify (*v.*)
-ic	ártist (*n.*)	artístic (*adj.*)
-atic	sýstem (*n.*)	systemátic (*adj.*)
-al	depártment (*n.*)	departméntal (*adj.*)
-ion	éducate (*v.*)	educátion (*n.*)
-ition	repéat (*v.*)	repetítion (*n.*)
-ation	invíte (*v.*)	invitátion (*n.*)
-cation	applý (*v.*)	applicátion (*n.*)

Practice the words below. In the first two columns the primary stress is on the same syllable. In column three, the stress is on a different syllable.

1.	2.	3.
élevate	élevator	elevátion
horízon	horízons	horizóntal
expériment	expérimenting	experiméntal
índicate	índicator	indícative
óperate	óperative	operátion
affírm	affírmative	affirmátion
oblíge	oblígatory	obligátion
sénse	sénsible	sensibílity

Practice these words. In the first column the primary stress is on the prefix; in the second column it is not.

1.	2.
súbway	subdúe
rébate	restárt
óversight	overtáke
íntake	implánt
tránslate	transáct
óutboard	outdáted
ántibody	anticlímax
nónsense	nonprófit

Exercise

Listen to the words below. Mark the primary stress of each word with a pencil. In some cases the primary stress is on the same syllable; in others it is not.

1. emphasis   emphatic   3. introduce   introduction
2. hemisphere   hemispherical   4. perfect   perfectly

5. condition   conditioning   10. imagine   imaginative
6. industry   industrious   11. conclude   conclusion
7. appreciate   appreciation   12. conclude   conclusive
8. lucky   luckily   13. valid   validity
9. imagine   imagination

Rhythm

Languages have rhythm or tempo. The kind of rhythm varies from language to language. In some there is a regular beat—da-da-da-da or da-DA-da-DA. In English the rhythm or timing can be said to be irregular. Many of the sentences in this book have been grouped together to help you gain a sense or "feel" of the rhythm of English.

In English the rhythm seems to be governed by the primary, secondary and tertiary stresses. The weak stressed words or syllables are very short and they are said very quickly. The addition of syllables with weak stress is made without disrupting the rhythm or adding to the total time it takes to say something.

In the following sentences notice that the rhythm is the same in each pair of sentences even though the second sentence has one more syllable with weak stress.

> Ann's book was new.   Ann's new hat is blue.
> Carol's book was old.   Jane's new hat is yellow.

In the sentences below, notice that the rhythm remains the same even though syllables with weak stress are in different places in the sentence.

> Ann's hat is yellow.   Elaine's hat is red.
> Carol's hat is blue.   Ann's jacket is lost.

In the following lines, notice that the rhythm is the same although there are different numbers of syllables with weak stress.

> Rain, rain, go away,   (4 stressed; 1 weak stress)
> Come again, another day.   (4 stressed; 3 weak stresses)

> Work, work.   (2 stressed; 0 weak stresses)
> Nothing but work,   (2 stressed; 2 weak stresses)
> Making beds,   (2 stressed; 1 weak stress)
> For travelling rabbits.   (2 stressed; 4 weak stresses)

In the following sentences, notice that the rhythm is changed by the addition of syllables with major stress but not by syllables with weak stress.

> Ann's hat is blue.   }
> Ann's hat is yellow. } same

> Ann's new hat is blue.} longer

> A ship sailed into the Red Sea.   }
> A steamer sailed into the Aegean Sea. } same

Á b̄ig sh̄ip sāiled īntȯ thė Ch̄inȧ Séa.
Á b̄ig sh̄ip sāiled īntȯ thė S̄outh Ch̄inȧ Séa. } longeı

Listen to these sentences and repeat them. Notice that the addition of syllables with weak stress in the second sentence of each group does not change the rhythm or add to the total time it takes to say the sentence. However, the addition of syllables with strong stress in sentences three and four of each group does change the rhythm and add to the time it takes to say them.

1. Thė b̄o̅ok is góod.   2.   Wh̄ere is Jóan?
    Thė m̄ovie is béttėr.   Wh̄ere is Cárȯl?

    Thė b̄ook is v̄erẏ bíg.   Wh̄ere is Jōan's cár?
    Thė b̄ook is qūite ínterėsting.   Wh̄ere is C̄arȯl's hóuse?

3. J̄ohn is ȧ sm̄art bóy.
    J̄ohnnẏ is ȧ dėp̄endȧblė wórkėr.

    J̄ohn is ȧ v̄erẏ sm̄art bóy.
    J̄ohnnẏ is ȧ v̄erẏ gōod wórkėr.

Practice Dialog 1

Mr. Johnson: Bíll, we'd l̄ike yōu tȯ c̄ome tȯ dínnėr n̄ext week.

Mr. White: Thánk yōu, Fréd.   Ī'd líke tȯ.

Mr. Johnson: Wōuld n̄ext Wédnesdȧy b̄e āll r̄ight?

Mr. White: Fíne.   Wh̄at tíme?

Mr. Johnson: S̄ix o'clóck.

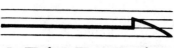

Mr. White: I'd better write that down.

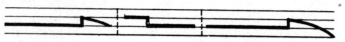

That's six o'clock, Wednesday, February sixteenth.

Mr. Johnson: Right.   Do you know where we live?

Mr. White: No, not exactly.

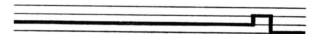

Mr. Johnson: The address is three-fourteen Maple Avenue.

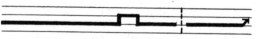

You know how to get there, don't you?

Mr. White: Yes.   It's just off Third Street, isn't it?

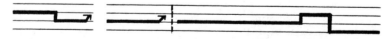

Mr. Johnson: That's right.   Very well. We'll see you next Wednesday.

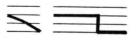

Mr. White: Fine.   Thank you.

Practice Dialog 2

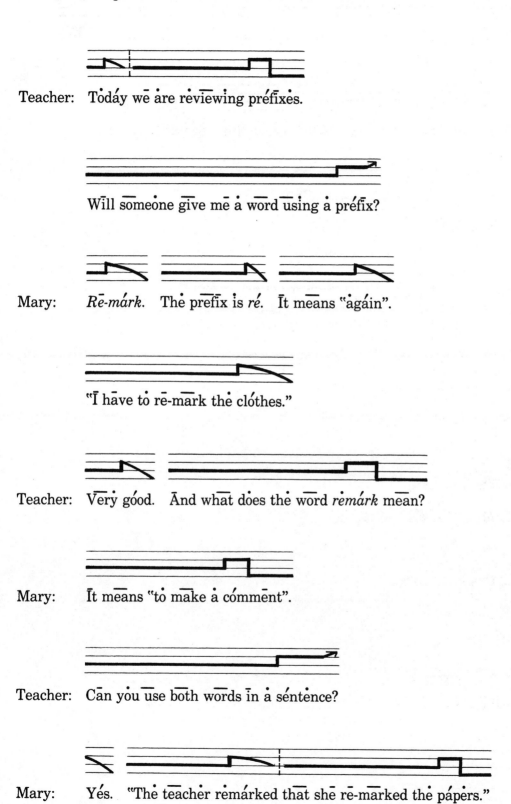

Teacher: Todáy we are reviewing préfixes.

Will someone give me a word using a préfix?

Mary: *Ré-márk*.   The prefix is *ré*.   It means "agáin".

"Í have to re-mark the clóthes."

Teacher: Véry góod.   And what does the word *remárk* mean?

Mary: Ít means "to make a cómment".

Teacher: Cán you use both words in a séntence?

Mary: Yés.   "The teacher remárked that she re-marked the pápers."

Teacher: Vĕrȳ góod.   Jóhn, căn yōu gīve mē ănóthĕr word ūsing thĕ *re* prefīx?

John: Yés.   *Rē-léase*.   Īt mēans "tó lēase sōmething ăgáin."

The wōrd *rĕléase* mēans "tó lĕt gó".

Teacher: Fíne.   Āre thĕre āny óthĕr pāirs ŏf words līke thīs?

Mary: *Rĕpréss* ănd *rē-préss*.

John: *Rĕláy* ănd *rē-láy*.

Mary: *Rĕfórm* ănd *rē-fórm*.

John: *Rĕfúnd* ănd *rē-fúnd*

Teacher: Thāt's vĕrȳ góod.

11. COMPREHENSION PRACTICE REDUCED FORMS ,

The drills which you have been practicing in this book have been marked for rather slow, careful speech.

When native Americans speak, however, the stresses in some cases would be a little different from those you have learned. This is especially true with certain kinds of words that have minor stress and which we have marked with tertiary stress, such as pronoun objects, certain verb forms and prepositions. A number of words or categories of words tend to have weak stress instead of tertiary stress. At the same time, these words often undergo a vowel change when under weak stress. We call words which are spoken with a weaker stress than normal and which have a vowel change — reductions. For example, in conversation, a native speaker would be likely to say

Ī héard 'im rather than *Ī héard hīm*. The writing system represents some of these reduced forms in certain standard ways, such as *'im* for *him*; *'er* for *her*; *'em* for *them*: *gonna* for *going to*. In order to comprehend English spoken by native speakers, it is necessary to have some familiarity with these forms. The basic intonation patterns you have been learning do not change in the manner that the stresses do.

This section will give you the opportunity to hear many of the reductions spoken at normal conversational speed.

Pronoun Subjects

Following auxiliaries and modals in questions   *(Tape 14 begins here.)*

We, I, she, they: These pronouns usually retain the same form, but they are often spoken with weak stress. *I* and *we* may combine with the auxiliary. That is, the auxiliary and the pronoun may be spoken with no pause between them so that they are spoken as one word: Examples:

> Am I invited?
> Do we know?
> Were we on time?
> Couldn't she go?
> Aren't they ready?

He /hiy/* usually becomes /iy/ and combines with the auxiliary. The hyphen (-) in the sentences below is used to show that two words are spoken as one. Examples: dóes-he /də́ziy/; did-it /dídit/.

Listen to both pairs of sentences below.

Slow, careful speech	*Rapid speech*
Does he know?	Does-he know?
Did he come?	Did-he come?
Is he gone?	Is-he gone?
Was he here?	Was-he here?
He doesn't know, does he?	He doesn't know, does-he?
He didn't come, did he?	He didn't come, did-he?
He could do it, couldn't he?	He could do it, couldn't-he?
He was here, wasn't he?	He was here, wasn't-he?

It /it/ usually combines with the auxiliary and has weak stress.

Slow, careful speech	*Rapid speech*
Did it arrive?	Did-it arrive?
Wasn't it easy?	Wasn't-it easy?
Has it come?	Has-it come?
Hasn't it arrived?	Hasn't-it arrived?
It's come, hasn't it?	It's come, hasn't-it?
It's here, isn't it?	It's here, isn't-it?

You /yuw/ often becomes /yə/ in rapid speech. The auxiliary *do* /duw/ when used before /yə/ is frequently pronounced /də/, giving /dəyə/.

Slow, careful speech	*Rapid speech*
Will you come?	Will-you come?
Can you go?	Can-you go?
Are you coming?	Are-you coming?
Do you know?	Do-you know?
Were you there?	Were-you there?

After the sound /d/, *you* may be pronounced /jə/ or /juw/. Examples: did-you /díjə/ or /díjuw/; could-you becomes /kújə/ or /kújuw/.

Could you hear?	Could-you hear?
Would you help?	Would-you help?
Did you know?	Did-you know?
Should you tell?	Should-you tell?
You couldn't do it, could you?	You couldn't do it, could-you?
You didn't tell him, did you?	You didn't tell him, did-you?

---

*For a summary of the phonemic symbols used in this lesson, please see page xvii.

After the sound /t/, *you* is usually pronounced /čə/ or /čuw/. Examples: don't-you /dónčə/ or /dównčuw/; haven't-you /hǽvənčə/ or /hǽvənčuw/.

Wōn't yŏu cóme?	Wōn't-yŏu cóme?
Don't you know?	Don't-you know?
Haven't you heard?	Haven't-you heard?
Couldn't you go?	Couldn't-you go?

Listen to these sentences spoken rapidly.

1. Why did-he go?	11. Don't-you know?
2. Did-he do it?	12. Couldn't-you do it?
3. Why can't-he come?	13. You're going, aren't-you?
4. Wouldn't-he help?	14. Haven't-you heard?
5. Does-it matter?	15. Won't-you try it?
6. Wouldn't-it go?	16. Would-you try?
7. Wasn't-it there?	17. Did-you go?
8. Hasn't-it arrived?	18. Where did-you go?
9. Is-it here?	19. Why did-you do it?
10. Was-it there?	20. You couldn't go, could-you?

Pronoun Objects

Me and *us* usually retain the same form, but they may be spoken with weak stress. *Us* may combine with the preceding verb.

Hē sáw mè.
They heard us.
They found me.
He wrote us.

Him /him/ usually becomes /im/ and combines with preceding verb.
Her /hər/ usually becomes /ər/ and combines with the verb.
It /it/ is spoken with weak stress and usually combines with the verb.
Listen to these sentences.

Slow, careful speech	*Rapid speech*
Ī héard hīm.	Ī héard-him.
We saw her.	We saw-her.
I did it.	I did-it.
We wrote him.	We wrote-him.
I told her.	I told-her.
He called her.	He called-her.

Them /ðem/ becomes /ðəm/ and may be spoken with weak stress. It may also lose the *th* sound and be spoken /əm/. This form, too, may combine with the verb.

Slow, careful speech	Rapid speech
Wē sáw thēm.	Wē sáw-thēm.
She wrote them a letter.	She wrote-them a letter.
I sold them a car.	I sold-them a car.
He told them last night.	He told-them last night.

You /yuw/ often becomes /yə/.

I'll pāy yōu tomórrŏw.	I'll pāy-yóu tomórrŏw.
He saw you downtown.	He saw-you downtown.
I'll show you.	I'll show-you.
He'll tell you the reason.	He'll tell-you the reason.

After the sound /t/ *you* is pronounced /čə/ or /čuw/.

Dīd it cút yōu?	Dīd it cút-yóu?
Did we forget you?	Did we forget-you?
I hope it didn't hurt you.	I hope it didn't hurt-you.
How much did it cost you?	How much did it cost-you?

After the sound /d/, *you* is pronounced /jə/ or /juw/.

Hē cálled yōu.	Hē cálled-yóu.
He'll lend you a dollar.	He'll lend-you a dollar.
He saved you some money.	He saved-you some money.
I told you so.	I told-you so.

Listen to these sentences spoken rapidly.

1. Glad to meet-you.
2. We heard-you speak.
3. Where did-you see-him?
4. When did-you call-her?
5. What did-he tell-them?

6. Why did-you do that?
7. Did-it hurt-you?
8. Where did-you see-us?
9. We heard-him talk.
10. I can't see-them.

Possessive Forms of Pronouns

The pronoun forms *your, his, her* are often spoken with weak stress and pronounced /yər/, /iz/, and /ər/. *Your,* when it follows the sound /d/ is usually pronounced /jər/; when it follows /t/, it becomes /čər/. Listen to the following sentences spoken rapidly.

1. Where's-his book?
2. What's-her address?
3. What's-your name?
4. Would-your sister know?
5. He doesn't know where-his book is.

6. Lend me your book.
7. I couldn't see-her face.
8. What's-his sister's name?
9. Did-your friend come?
10. I'm sorry. I lost-your book.

Question Words

After question words like *who, when, where, why,* the auxiliary *did* often becomes simply /d/. Certain pronoun forms combine with the /d/, and the whole expression of question word—did—pronoun is spoken as though it were one word. The final /t/ of *what*, also, is frequently lost when this word is next to *did*, and only the /d/ of the auxiliary is heard. Listen to the following.

Where-did-he go?	/h͞werdiy gów/
Why-did-you do-it?	/h͞wayjə dúwit/
When-did-it happen?	/h͞wendit hǽpen/
Who-did-he ask?	/h͞uwdiy ǽsk/
What-did-he do?	/h͞wadiy dúw/
Why-did-you go?	/h͞wayjuw gów/
When-did-you tell her?	/h͞wenjə télər/
Where-did-you see-it?	/h͞werjə siýit/
Why-did-he do that?	/h͞waydiy dúw ðǽt/
What-did-I tell you?	/h͞waday tél yūw/

Listen also to the following sentences which use question words with a form of the verb *be*.

Where-are-you going?	/h͞weryə góiŋ/
What's-he reading?	/h͞watsiy riýdiŋ/
Why-are-you stopping?	/h͞wayəryə stápiŋ/
When-is-he coming?	/h͞wenziy kə́miŋ/
Who-is-he calling?	/h͞uwziy kɔ́liŋ/

Verb Forms

Have—as an auxiliary in compound verb phrases

In verb phrases such as *I could have gone,* the word *have* is often pronounced /əv/ or /ə/ with weak stress.

Slow, careful speech	*Rapid speech*
I c͞ould h͞ave góne.	I could-have góne.
You shouldn't have told me.	You shouldn't-have told me.
He wouldn't have known.	He wouldn't-have known.
I could have told you.	I could-have told you.

Verbs—ending in *-ing.*

In rapid speech, it is common to hear the final *-ing* of verbs spoken as /in/.

Where are you going?	Where are you goin'?
What are you doing?	What are you doin'?
Are you leaving?	Are you leavin'?
They're playing tennis.	They're playin' tennis.

Want to: This is often pronounced as /wántə/ or /wánə/.

Have to and *Has to:* These forms are generally spoken as /hǽftə/ and /hǽstə/.

Got to: This is usually pronounced /gátə/.

Ought to: This is commonly pronounced /ɔ́tə/.

Going to: When used as an auxiliary, several forms are heard /gówiŋtə/, /gówintə/ and /gónə/.

Slow, careful speech	Rapid speech
We're going to dó it.	We're going-to dó it.
I don't want to go.	I don't want-to go.
We'll have to do it.	We'll have-to do it.
He's got to study.	He's got-to study.
Do you want to try it?	Do you want-to try it?

Listen to these sentences.

1. Where do you want to go?
2. What are you going to do?
3. When is he going to come?
4. I don't think they're going to come.
5. Does he have to study?

6. I didn't want to do it.
7. He isn't going to pass.
8. He doesn't want to drive.
9. He has to go home early.
10. I think you ought to do it.

Prepositions

Certain prepositions also have reduced forms when they are pronounced with weak stress.

Of: This preposition is used with containers and units of measurement. It is usually pronounced /ə/ and is joined to the preceding noun. Before a following vowel sound, it is commonly pronounced /əv/. Listen to these examples.

Slow, careful speech	Rapid speech
cup of cóffee	cup-of cóffee
glass of milk	glass-of milk
carton of eggs	carton-of eggs
pitcher of water	pitcher-of water
can of fruit	can-of fruit
pound of butter	pound-of butter
quart of milk	quart-of milk
yard of cloth	yard-of cloth
full of water	full-of water
a lot of sand	a lot-of sand

At: This is often spoken with weak stress and is pronounced /ət/.

at hóme	at hóme
at school	at school
at noon	at noon
at midnight	at midnight
at work	at work
at ten o'clock	at ten o'clock

For: This is pronounced /fər/ with weak stress, when the following noun or pronoun is stressed.

fōr mé	for mé
for him	for him
for John	for John
for two dollars	for two dollars

Listen to these sentences.

1. Please give me a cup of coffee.
2. I'd like a quart of milk, please.
3. It's full of water!
4. I have a lot of those.
5. I bought a can of corn, a bottle of milk, and a carton of eggs.
6. I think she's at home.
7. I did it for John.
8. I'll see you at ten o'clock.
9. My father's at work.
10. He'll be home at midnight.

Listen to the following conversations in which a number of reduced forms of all types are used. The reduced forms are shown in italics.

A. Tom: *Come here* a minute.
   Fred: *What do you* want?
   Tom: I *want to* see your hat.
   Fred: What's the matter with it?
   Tom: Nothing. *Did it* cost much?
   Fred: No, not much.

B. Bill: I *have to* catch a train.
   Jim: *Where are you going?*
   Bill: I'm *going to* Washington.
   Jim: *What are you going* there for?
   Bill: I'm *going to* visit my cousin.

C. Mary: You're Frank, *aren't you?*
   Frank: Yes. *How'd you* know?
   Mary: Sally told me.
   Frank: Oh. *Did she* come tonight?
   Mary: Yes. *Haven't you* seen *her* yet?

D. Mother: *What are you doing*, June?
   June: Nothing, Mother. *What do you* want?
   Mother: *Could you* go to the store for me?
   June: I'd be glad to. *Do you* have a list?
   Mother: No. You'll *have to* make one.
   June: All right. I'm ready.
   Mother: I need *a pound of* coffee, *a quart of* milk, and *a loaf of* bread.
   June: Is that all?

Mother: No. Get two *cans of* corn, *a bottle of* catsup, *a head of* lettuce, and *a jar of* pickles.
            I think that's all.

June: O.K. I'll be right back.

E. Mr. Green: Hi, Tom. Why *weren't you* at the meeting last night?

Mr. White: I *had to* work. *How did it* go?

Mr. Green: O.K., I guess.
            Are you going bowling tonight?

Mr. White: No. I'm not *going to* go.
            I *have to* work again.

Mr. Green: Why *don't you* take a little time off?
            You *ought to* get some exercise, you know.

Mr. White: I know. But we'll be finished with this project tomorrow.
            Then I'll be free again.

Mr. Green: *Have you* eaten *lunch yet*?

Mr. White: No. I'm not *going to* eat today.
            I'll buy *you a cup of* coffee though.

Mr. Green: O.K. Let's go.

WORD LIST

A few of the most productive word stress patterns are illustrated below. Also listed are numerous examples of two-word verbs and noun compounds. In some lists examples of nouns, verbs and adjectives are given separately; in others they are grouped together alphabetically. Some words, of course, have variant pronunciations and differing stress patterns. These words are not singled out in the lists. *Mustache*, for example, appears in the primary-tertiary list as /məstǽš/; *program* in the same list as /prówgræm/. The fact that they may be also pronounced /məstǽš/ and /prówgrəm/ is not noted.

A very few examples of adjective and verb compounds with primary stress on the first element appear at the end of the listings.

All lists, of course, are far from exhaustive.

The table below shows the patterns that are illustrated in the lists.

List No.	Pattern	List No.	Pattern
1	′	13	• ,•–
2	,•	14	– ,•
3	,••	15	– • ,
4	,•••	16	– • ,•
5	•,	17	, – (noun compounds)
6	•,•	18	,• – ″ ″
7	•,••	19	, – • ″ ″
8	•,•••	20	,• – • ″ ″
9	,–	21	, •– • ″ ″
10	– ,	22	•,• – ″ ″
11	,•–	23	Longer forms of noun compounds
12	,•– •	24	Various verb compounds
		25	Various adjective compounds

List 1: ′

Nouns

age	band	boat	bread	cake	chair	church	cloud	cow
arm	bank	book	breath	cap	check	class	coast	cup
art	bed	bowl	breeze	car	cheese	clerk	coat	dance
aunt	bird	box	brush	card	chest	clock	coin	day
bag	blouse	boy	bus	cat	child	clothes	comb	desk

107

dish	knee	sheep	bathe	guess	pay	swim	dim	**new**
dog	lake	shirt	beg	guide	phone	take	dry	nice
door	lamp	shoe	break	hang	play	talk	dull	odd
dress	leg	sign	bring	hate	point	teach	fair	old
ear	life	silk	brush	have	pour	think	far	pale
egg	light	snow	build	hear	print	throw	fast	plain
eye	line	soap	burn	help	prove	turn	fat	poor
face	list	song	buy	hit	pull	type	fine	proud
fact	lock	soup	call	hold	push	use	firm	pure
farm	lunch	spoon	cause	hope	put	vote	flat	queer
field	man	stair	charge	hurt	race	wait	frank	rare
fire	match	star	close	join	rain	walk	fresh	raw
fish	meal	store	cost	keep	read	want	full	red
flood	mile	storm	cough	kill	rent	wash	gay	rich
floor	milk	street	count	kiss	roll	wear	glad	rude
flute	month	suit	cross	know	run	wish	good	safe
fork	moon	sun	cure	laugh	sail	work	grand	sane
form	name	tape	cut	leave	say	write	gray	sharp
friend	neck	tea	dance	lend	see		great	short
fun	niece	tooth	die	lift	send	*Adjectives*	green	sick
game	nose	town	do	light	serve	bad	grim	slow
glass	nurse	train	doubt	like	share	big	hard	small
glove	page	tree	dress	live	shout	black	high	smart
golf	pen	week	drink	lock	show	blue	hot	soft
guest	pie	wife	drive	look	sit	bright	just	stiff
hair	pig	wind	drop	lose	ski	broad	kind	straight
hand	pipe	wool	dry	love	sleep	brown	lame	strange
head	plan	world	eat	mail	smoke	cheap	large	strong
health	plane	wrist	fall	make	snow	clean	late	sweet
heart	price	year	feel	match	solve	clear	lean	tall
heat	race		fight	mean	speak	cold	light	thick
home	rain	*Verbs*	find	meet	spell	cool	long	thin
horse	rice	ache	fit	miss	spend	crude	loose	vast
house	rose	act	fix	move	stand	damp	mad	warm
job	salt	add	get	need	start	dark	mean	wet
juice	sea	aid	give	owe	state	dear	mild	wide
key	seat	ask	go	own	stay	deep	moist	wild
			grow	pass	stop	dense	neat	young

List 2: ⌒

Nouns

acid	army	breakfast	ceiling	daughter	error	hunger	letter	money
actor	arrow	brother	circus	dentist	factor	husband	lettuce	morning
actress	artist	building	city	diet	farmer	item	market	mother
agent	autumn	bushel	climate	dinner	father	kettle	medal	mountain
anchor	baby	butter	coffee	distance	favor	kitchen	member	movie
angle	baggage	button	cottage	doctor	finger	lady	message	music
ankle	barber	cabbage	cotton	doctrine	flower	language	method	neighbor
answer	basis	camel	cousin	drama	garden	lawyer	minute	nephew
apple	bottle	captain	country	driver	grammar	leather	mirror	ocean
apron	bracelet	carrot	credit	engine	horror	lesson	moment	office

onion
orange
orbit
package
painter
palace
paper
parent
partner
pastry
pencil
people
person
picture
pleasure
postage
promise
question
rattle
razor
reason
record
rival
river
rumor
sailor
scissors
season
secret
sentence
shoulder
signal
sister
soldier
sorrow
station
stocking
story
stranger
student
sugar
summer
supper
sweater
swimmer
symbol
system
table
tailor
taxi
teacher

tennis
ticket
towel
tractor
traffic
trouble
uncle
unit
valley
victim
visit
wagon
waiter
water
weapon
weather
wedding
window
winter
woman
worker

Noun Plurals

ages
blouses
boxes
breezes
brushes
buses
children
churches
classes
dances
dishes
dresses
faces
glasses
horses
houses
kisses
lunches
matches
nieces
noses
nurses
oxen
pages
pieces
prices
races

roses

Verbs

alter
anger
answer
argue
bandage
banish
battle
blossom
blunder
border
borrow
bother
budget
burden
bury
button
cable
capture
carry
caution
challenge
cherish
circle
comfort
comment
counsel
credit
damage
differ
doctor
edit
empty
enter
envy
equal
exit
fasten
favor
figure
finish
flatter
flavor
flourish
flower
follow
function
furnish

gamble
garden
gossip
grumble
hammer
handle
happen
harvest
hasten
hinder
honor
hurry
launder
lecture
limit
listen
manage
market
marry
master
measure
mention
merit
mingle
motion
murder
mutter
notice
nourish
offer
open
orbit
package
pardon
perish
picnic
pilot
polish
practice
profit
promise
punish
question
ruin
service
settle
signal
soften
sparkle
steady
struggle

study
suffer
travel
trouble
utter
value
vanish
visit
welcome
whisper
whistle
wonder
worry

Verbs
ing-form

asking
bringing
building
buying
calling
counting
doing
driving
finding
fixing
getting
going
guessing
helping
holding
keeping
laughing
looking
paying
putting
sleeping
speaking
taking
teaching
working
etc.

Verbs: Form ending in /t/ or /d/

acted
added
aided

counted
doubted
guided
hated
landed
lifted
lighted
needed
pointed
printed
rented
shouted
started
stated
voted
waited
wanted
etc.

Verbs: Form ending in a Sibilant

brushes
causes
charges
closes
crosses
dances
dresses
fixes
guesses
kisses
loses
matches
misses
passes
pushes
races
teaches
uses
washes
wishes

brilliant
busy
careful
certain
charming
clever
cloudy
crowded
dirty
easy
famous
fluent
formal
gentle
happy
healthy
heavy
honest
hungry
idle
jealous
juicy
little
local
lonely
loyal
modern
noisy
perfect
pleasant
pretty
proper
purple
quiet
ready
royal
sacred
simple
sleepy
slender
sober
sorry
sunny
thirsty
useful
yellow

Adjectives

able
active
angry
anxious
bitter

Adjectives: Comparative and Superlative Forms

bigger

bluer
brighter
cheaper
colder
darker
deeper
dimmer
drier
faster
flatter
fresher
greater
harder
kinder
larger
milder
nicer
richer
safer
smaller
taller
biggest
brightest
cheapest
hottest
newest

Other Words

after
any
barely
cheaply
ever
largely
loudly
nearly
never
often
only
other
over
quickly
rather
sadly
seldom
slowly
softly
under
very

List 3: ´ · ·

Nouns				Adjectives	Adjectives: Comparative and Superlative Forms

Nouns

accident
admiral
animal
area
article
audience
calendar
carpenter
cereal
champion
chocolate
citizen
company
confidence
continent
creditor
criminal
customer
elephant
emptiness
evidence
factory
favorite
foreigner
formula
frequency
furniture
gardener
general
gentleman
gentleness
government
handkerchief
hospital
incident
instrument
jeweler
management
measurement
medicine
messenger
mineral
misery
mystery
nourishment
officer

orchestra
ornament
oxygen
parliament
passenger
period
physicist
president
principal
property
providence
punishment
quantity
radio
remedy
royalty
sentiment
settlement
signature
specialist
spectacle
stadium
sympathy
theater
tragedy
usefulness
vegetable
visitor
wilderness

Noun plurals

actresses
bandages
cabbages
challenges
circuses
cottages
damages
distances
images
languages
messages
notices
oranges
packages
promises
seamstresses

sentences
services

Verbs: ing-form

answering
arguing
borrowing
bothering
butchering
buttoning
carrying
comforting
covering
doctoring
entering
favoring
featuring
finishing
flowering
following
gardening
happening
harvesting
hurrying
listening
marrying
numbering
opening
ordering
packaging
pardoning
picturing
practicing
promising
publishing
questioning
servicing
shouldering
showering
softening
soldiering
studying
thundering
traveling
visiting
wandering

welcoming
wondering
worrying

Verbs: Form ending in a sibilant

bandages
banishes
challenges
cherishes
damages
finishes
flourishes
furnishes
harnesses
manages
menaces
notices
nourishes
packages
perishes
polishes
practices
promises
publishes
punishes
sentences
services
surfaces
vanishes

Verbs: Form ending in /t/ or /d/

budgeted
comforted
credited
dieted
edited
exited
harvested
marketed
merited
orbited
piloted
visited

Adjectives

average
beautiful
critical
curious
dangerous
definite
desperate
different
excellent
favorite
federal
fortunate
glorious
gradual
ignorant
innocent
intimate
lavender
liberal
marvelous
medical
mountainous
musical
natural
negative
obvious
opposite
passionate
permanent
personal
physical
popular
possible
powerful
practical
principal
probable
prominent
radical
sensible
serious
several
terrible
tropical
wonderful

Adjectives: Comparative and Superlative Forms

angrier
busier
cleverer
cloudier
dirtier
easier
happier
healthier
heavier
hungrier
juicier
lonelier
noisier
pleasanter
prettier
quieter
sleepier
slenderer
sorrier
thirstier
yellower

angriest
busiest
cleverest

Adverbs

angrily
carefully
easily
faithfully
fluently
frequently
helpfully
luckily
perfectly
possibly
privately
readily
terribly
thankfully
thoughtfully
truthfully
usefully

List 4: ′ · · ·

amicable	generously	miniature	permanently	questionable	serviceable
amicably	gentlemanly	miserable	personally	radiantly	similarly
casually	honorable	miserably	pleasurable	rapturously	temperature
definitely	innocently	moderately	powerfully	reasonably	variously
formidable	manageable	naturally	practicable	relatively	violently
formidably	marriageable	negatively	preferable	separately	virtuously
fortunately	menacingly	perishable	publishable	seriously	wonderfully

List 5: · ′

Nouns	exchange	today	become	divide	perform
	excuse	tonight	begin	elapse	permit
abuse	expense		believe	elect	possess
accord	extent	*Verbs*	belong	embrace	predict
account	fatigue		collapse	emerge	prepare
address	garage	abuse	collect	employ	present
advice	guitar	accept	compel	endure	pretend
affair	Japan	accuse	complain	engage	prevent
alarm	July	achieve	complete	enjoy	produce
amount	lament	acquaint	conceal	equip	promote
attempt	machine	acquire	conclude	erase	pronounce
award	mistake	adapt	confess	escape	protect
balloon	neglect	adjourn	confuse	exchange	provide
belief	offense	adjust	consent	excite	recall
Brazil	parade	agree	consist	exclaim	receive
command	perfume	allow	consume	excuse	recite
complaint	Peru	amaze	contain	exist	record
concern	police	amend	control	expect	reduce
consent	pursuit	amuse	converse	explain	refer
control	receipt	announce	convince	explore	regret
debate	reform	annoy	correct	express	relax
decay	regret	appeal	debate	forget	release
defeat	relief	appear	decide	forgive	remain
defense	remark	applaud	delay	ignore	remark
degree	reply	apply	demand	improve	remind
delay	report	appoint	depart	inform	repair
delight	request	approach	depend	inquire	repeat
demand	research	approve	despise	insist	reply
design	response	arrange	destroy	inspect	report
desire	result	arrest	detect	instruct	research
despair	retreat	arrive	deter	insure	reserve
dessert	return	assign	devote	invent	retreat
device	revenge	assist	devour	invite	return
disease	reverse	assume	direct	involve	reveal
disgrace	review	assure	discuss	neglect	select
disguise	reward	attack	disguise	obey	suggest
disgust	sedan	attend	dismiss	observe	suppose
dispute	success	attract	display	obtain	surprise
effect	support	avoid	dispute	offend	surround
escape	surprise	award	disturb	oppose	survey

suspect	abrupt	alike	aside	between	extreme
suspend	absurd	alive	asleep	beyond	hello
	across	alone	awake	complete	instead
Other Words	acute	along	away	confused	perhaps
	afraid	aloud	because	correct	polite
aboard	again	among	before	corrupt	refined
about	ago	apart	behind	direct	severe
above	ahead	around	below	distinct	superb
abroad	alert	ashamed	beside	enough	until
				exact	upon

List 6: • ´ •

Nouns				*Verbs: Form ending in a Sibilant*	perplexes
	equipment	solution	entitle		possesses
	eraser	suggestion	establish		produces
addition	example	suspicion	examine		professes
advantage	exception	tobacco	imagine	abuses	progresses
affection	explorer	tomato	inhabit	accuses	pronounces
agreement	horizon	tomorrow	inherit	addresses	proposes
Alaska	improvement	tradition	initial	advises	reduces
allowance	infection	vanilla	interpret	alleges	refreshes
amusement	inspection		prohibit	amazes	refuses
apartment	instruction	*Noun plurals*	remember	amuses	relaxes
appearance	intention		resemble	approaches	releases
appliance	investment	addresses	surrender	arises	replaces
appointment	mechanic	disguises		arranges	reproaches
Atlantic	Morocco	exchanges		attaches	revenges
attendant	musician	excuses	*Verbs:*	beseeches	reverses
attention	objection	garages	*ing form*	collapses	revises
banana	occasion	offenses		commences	suppresses
behavior	official	responses	accepting	confesses	surprises
collection	opinion	reverses	accusing	converses	
committee	pajamas	surprises	agreeing	convinces	*Verbs: Form*
companion	permission		amusing	despises	*ending in*
conclusion	petition	*Verbs*	announcing	discusses	*/t/ or /d/*
condition	physician		appearing	disguises	
conductor	piano	abandon	appointing	dismisses	
confession	policeman	accomplish	arriving	divorces	accepted
connection	possession	accustom	attending	embraces	accorded
construction	potato	astonish	avoiding	emerges	accounted
convention	prevention	awaken	becoming	encloses	acquainted
December	production	bewilder	beginning	enforces	adapted
decision	profession	commission	believing	engages	adjusted
department	professor	consider	belonging	erases	admitted
depression	proportion	continue	confusing	exchanges	adopted
destruction	proposal	deliver	correcting	excuses	afforded
detective	provision	deposit	deciding	exposes	amended
diploma	reception	determine	demanding	expresses	amounted
direction	recorder	develop	discussing	impresses	appointed
disaster	reporter	discover	enjoying	increases	assented
division	religion	distinguish	forgetting	induces	assisted
dominion	republic	embarrass	improving	indulges	attempted
election	resistance	encounter	permitting	opposes	attended
emotion	selection	encourage	preparing	oppresses	attracted
employment	sensation	endeavor	receiving		avoided

collected	divided	instructed	regretted	attractive	peculiar
commanded	elected	intended	reminded	confusing	persistent
concluded	encouraged	invented	repeated	convenient	productive
conducted	endeavored	invested	reported	delicious	protective
conflicted	erected	invited	requested	delightful	receptive
consented	exceeded	lamented	resented	destructive	romantic
constructed	excepted	neglected	resisted	distinctive	successful
contented	exerted	objected	respected	domestic	sufficient
contrasted	exhausted	offended	responded	effective	surprising
converted	existed	paraded	rewarded	efficient	suspicious
corrected	expanded	permitted	selected	electric	tremendous
corrupted	expected	persuaded	submitted	enormous	
debated	expended	predicted	subtracted	essential	*Other Words*
decided		presented	suggested	exciting	
defeated	*Verbs: Form*	pretended	surrounded	exhaustive	abruptly
defended	*ending in*	prevented	suspected	expensive	another
demanded	*/t/ or /d/*	projected	suspended	extensive	completely
departed		promoted		external	correctly
depended	excited	protected	*Adjectives*	familiar	directly
deported	exploded	protested		financial	diversely
descended	exploited	provided	abundant	important	exactly
deserted	extended	reacted	aggressive	indignant	extremely
detected	imported	recorded	amusing	objective	precisely
devoted	included	reflected	apparent	offensive	together
directed	inspected	regarded	artistic		

List 7: ·′··

Nouns	encouragement	superior	embarrasses	depositing	deliberate
	environment	thermometer	establishes	determining	disposable
ability	establishment	variety		developing	electrical
academy	executive	vicinity	*Verbs: Form*	discovering	exceptional
accessory	experience		*ending in*	distinguishing	excitable
accomplishment	experiment	*Noun Plurals*	*/t/ or /d/*	embarrassing	expandable
activity	exterior			encountering	exploitable
ambassador	extremity	acquaintances	contributed	encouraging	extendable
analysis	facility	advantages	deposited	establishing	forgivable
apology	ingredient	allegiances	exhibited	examining	immediate
artillery	inhabitant	allowances	inhabited	inheriting	industrious
associate	intelligence	appearances	inherited	interpreting	inferior
astonishment	interior	appliances	interpreted	prohibiting	inflammable
bewilderment	legality		prohibited	remembering	intelligent
capacity	majority	*Verbs*		surrendering	intentional
certificate	material		*Verbs—*		legitimate
commodity	memorial	accompany	*ing-form*	*Adjectives*	magnificent
community	necessity	experiment			mechanical
comparison	pedestrian		abandoning	additional	meticulous
confederate	phenomenon	*Verbs*	accomplishing	adventuresome	obedient
conservative	philosopher	*Ending in a*	astonishing	appropriate	observable
continuance	photographer	*Sibilant*	awakening	available	occasional
development	proprietor		bewildering	conceivable	original
discoverer	security	accomplishes	considering	conservative	particular
embarrassment	society	astonishes	continuing	debatable	pertetual
emergency	stenographer	distinguishes	delivering	defensible	pictorial

political	tyrannical	conceivably	efficiently	indignantly	pretentiously
presentable		confusedly	enormously	initially	prophetically
preventable	*Adverbs*	conveniently	especially	instinctively	protectingly
professional		convincingly	essentially	internally	protectively
proportionate	abundantly	deceivingly	eternally	invitingly	religiously
remarkable	aggressively	decreasingly	exceedingly	mechanically	remarkably
removable	amusedly	defensibly	excitedly	objectively	romantically
repairable	amusingly	deliciously	exhaustively	officially	statistically
responsible	apparently	delightfully	externally	peculiarly	successfully
reversable	assumedly	destructively	familiarly	permissively	sufficiently
ridiculous	attractively	domestically	importantly	persistently	surprisingly
superior	beseechingly	effectively	increasingly	politically	suspiciously
					tremendously

List 8:   • ′ • • •

additionally	considerably	distributively	inevitable	mysteriously	particularly
affectionately	considerately	emotionally	inevitably	obediently	pictorially
appropriately	contractually	encouragingly	informatively	objectionable	professionally
companionable	cooperative	exceptionally	inhabitable	objectionably	proportionately
comparatively	deliberately	immediately	intelligible	occasionally	provisionally
conditionally	determinedly	impressionable	intentionally	originally	traditionally
considerable	distinguishable	industriously	magnificently		

List 9:   ′ ‾

Nouns	carbide	contract	extract	instinct	tripod
	charcoal	convent	feline	invoice	trombone
abstract	co-ed	convoy	female	mustache	welfare
accent	cognac	costume	finance	nitrate	
access	cohort	curfew	format	nylon	*Verbs*
address	combat	cyclone	glucose	orlon	
adult	combine	dacron	graphite	platform	bisect
adverb	compact	decrease	hemlock	probate	broadcast
afghan	complex	Denmark	impact	process	collate
ampere	compound	dentine	impasse	profile	create
apex	compress	digest	import	program	dilate
archive	conclave	discard	imprint	pronoun	export
aspect	concord	discharge	impulse	protein	filtrate
athlete	conduct	discord	incense	protest	foment
Aztec	confab	discount	incline	proton	import
biceps	confine	discourse	income	replay	migrate
biped	conflict	duplex	increase	retake	probate
biplane	console	empire	index	surplus	profile
bivalve	consort	endive	influx	suspect	program
bombast	contact	escort	inquest	torment	prostrate
boycott	content	excise	insect	transcript	rotate
burlap	contest	exile	insert	transfer	translate
caisson	context	exploit	insight	transport	vibrate
canton	contour	export	insole		

List 10: ‾ ′

Nouns	misname	rebuild	remount	bring on	give back
	misquote	reboil	rename	bring out	hand in
Bastille	mistrust	recheck	repack	bring to	hang up
brochure	nonplus	reclean	repaint	bring up	hold up
campaign	postpone	recomb	rephrase	brush off	keep up
cartoon	transact	recook	replant	brush out	leave out
cascade	transcend	recut	replay	burn down	look up
cashier	transcribe	redo	resell	burn up	make out
chateau	transmit	redraft	reset	buy out	pay back
Chinese	transpire	refilm	reshow	call off	pick up
cliché	transplant	refit	resow	call up	point out
rebirth	transport	refund	restack	calm down	put on
routine	undo	reglue	retake	cheer up	ring up
technique	unlock	regrade	rewind	chop down	sell out
	unpack	regrind	reword	clean out	show off
Verbs	unseal	regrow	rework	clear off	slow down
	withdraw	reheat		close down	spell out
bombard	withhold	rehouse	*Two-Word*	count in	take off
compact	withstand	reknit	*Verbs*	cross out	tear up
maintain		release		cut down	try on
miscall	*Verbs—With*	relight	add up	draw up	turn in
miscast	*Prefix "Re"*	reload	back up	drive back	turn on
miscount	*Meaning "Again"*	remark	bawl out	eat up	use up
misguide		remelt	blow up	fill out	wear out
mismatch	rebind	remix	break down	find out	wind up

List 11: ′ · ‾

Nouns	enterprise	substitute	classify	graduate	operate
	envelope	telegram	compensate	gratify	pacify
acrobat	exercise	telegraph	complicate	hesitate	paralyze
alcohol	gasoline	telephone	compromise	illustrate	penetrate
alkali	handicap	telescope	concentrate	imitate	qualify
alphabet	holiday	uniform	constitute	immigrate	realize
altitude	institute	universe	contemplate	implement	recognize
appetite	interview		criticize	indicate	regulate
astronaut	latitude	*Verbs*	cultivate	interview	sacrifice
atmosphere	magazine		decorate	intimate	satisfy
attitude	magistrate	advertise	dedicate	irritate	specify
avalanche	merchandise	advocate	demonstrate	isolate	stimulate
benefit	millionaire	agitate	dominate	justify	substitute
boulevard	multitude	alternate	educate	legislate	telegraph
candidate	paradise	analyze	elevate	magnify	telephone
catalogue	paragraph	benefit	estimate	manifest	terrorize
circumstance	photograph	calculate	execute	multiply	testify
compromise	politics	celebrate	exercise	nominate	violate
democrat	sacrifice	civilize	fascinate	notify	

List 12: ′ · ‾ ·

agriculture	dictionary	hortatory	missionary	secondary	tertiary
allegory	dormitory	laboratory	oratory	secretary	visionary
cemetery	dromedary	laudatory	ordinary	television	voluntary
complicated	elevator	military	planetary		

List 13: · ′ · ‾

abbreviate	anticipate	associate	elaborate	exaggerate	originate
accommodate	apologize	communicate	eliminate	illuminate	participate
accumulate	appreciate	congratulate			

List 14: ‾ ′ ·

abnormal	foundation	outstanding	transparent	vacation
athletic	gigantic	sensation	umbrella	

List 15: ‾ · ′

absolute	ascertain	engineer	introduce	overlook	underneath
afternoon	disappear	gasoline	overcome	overtake	understand
apropos	disappoint	guarantee	overhead	overthrow	undertake

List 16: ‾ · ′ ·

absolutely	annotation	complication	engineering	independent	patriotic
academic	apparatus	concentration	execution	indication	population
admonition	application	constitution	expedition	information	propaganda
adoration	apprehension	contemplation	explanation	introduction	punctuation
advantageous	aromatic	conversation	fascination	irritation	recreation
adventitious	artificial	corporation	fundamental	isolation	regulation
advertisement	automatic	cultivation	generation	legislation	revolution
affectation	aviation	decoration	graduation	limitation	satisfaction
affidavit	calculation	democratic	hesitation	locomotive	stimulation
agitation	celebration	economic	illustration	manufacture	superstition
allegretto	compensation	education	imitation	nomination	universal
analytic	competition	elevation	independence	operation	violation

Noun Compounds

List 17: ′ ‾

airplane	bedtime	bran flakes	darkroom	eyelid	gold mine
airport	birdhouse	bus stop	day school	farm hand	golf bag
armchair	birthplace	chest cold	doorbell	farmhouse	golf balls
ashtray	blackbird	chopsticks	downfall	file clerk	golf clubs
backache	blackboard	classroom	dress shirt	fire chief	grade school
ballroom	bluebird	coal mine	drugstore	fireplace	grape juice
bank clerk	bookstore	cornflakes	earache	football	greenhouse
bathroom	boxcar	dance hall	earthquake	fruit juice	hairbrush

haircut	ice skates	notebook	road map	soup spoon	teaspoon
hairdo	lifeboat	oil well	rowboat	spaceship	test tube
handbag	light bulbs	pancakes	school books	sport shirt	textbook
handball	lighthouse	passport	schoolboy	steak knife	tiepin
hand cream	lunchroom	ping-pong	seashore	steamship	toothache
headache	mailbox	plane trip	shipwreck	stopwatch	toothpaste
high school	mailman	popcorn	shoe store	streetcar	topcoat
highway	mail truck	racehorse	ski poles	suitcase	toy store
horseback	mouthwash	racetrack	snowman	suitcoat	track shoes
horse race	necktie	railroad	snowshoes	sunrise	washcloth
houseguest	newsstand	raincoat	snowstorm	sweetheart	weekend
housewife	night school	rain hat	soup bowl	teapot	wineglass
				tearoom	wristwatch

List 18: ′ · ‾

apple tree	carving knife	fingerprint	nursery school	rifle range	tablespoon
baggage car	chewing gum	fishing rod	orange juice	riverbank	tabletop
barbershop	chocolate bar	flower shop	overcoat	riverboat	tennis balls
basketball	clothing store	fountain pen	paper boy	roller skates	tennis court
bathing suit	coffee cream	grammar book	parking lot	salad fork	textile mill
beauty shop	coffee cup	grocery store	parking space	shaving cream	thunderstorm
bowling ball	cookie jar	hiding place	picture book	shower soap	traffic light
bowling shoes	dairy barn	hobby shop	playing cards	steering wheel	underwear
boxing gloves	dinner plate	language school	pocketknife	storybook	volleyball
boxing ring	dressing gown	laundry room	postage stamp	sugar bowl	waiting room
butcher's shop	fairy tale	living room	problem child	summertime	water glass
butter knife	fencing mask	meeting place	punching bag	swimming pool	water skis
camping gear	ferris wheel	movie star	razor blades	swimming suit	weatherman
candy store	fingernail	music box	riding horse	tablecloth	wedding bells

List 19: ′ ‾ ·

bath powder	clothes closet	gunpowder	meat platter	saleslady	teakettle
blackberry	coat hanger	hair tonic	milk bottle	saltshaker	timetable
blood pressure	cream pitcher	hand lotion	newspaper	schoolteacher	truck driver
bookkeeper	dressmaker	handwriting	outpatient	sea level	typewriter
bullfighting	ear doctor	horse racing	pineapple	shoemaker	wastebasket
bus driver	eyeglasses	ice skating	post office	soup ladle	watchmaker
cabdriver	fire engine	light fixture	racehorses	stock market	wheelbarrow
church steeple	gas station	matchfolder	rose garden		

List 20: ′ · ‾ ·

army rations	doctor's office	flower garden	mountain climber	science teacher	
beauty parlor	drama critic	garden party	music teacher	storyteller	
business client	drinking fountain	grammar lesson	office worker	swimming practice	
chapter heading	engine trouble	heating system	pepper shaker	tennis racquet	
city dweller	English teacher	honor student	picnic table	tissue paper	
cleaning fluid	factory worker	horror story	prison sentence	trumpet player	
dancing partner	fairy story	language teacher	record changer	water faucet	
dentist's office	figure skating	mischief-maker	rental agent	water-skiing	
dinner hour	filling station	moneylender	rocket launcher	wrapping paper	
				writing paper	

List 21: ′ ˙ ⁻ ˙

art collector	flood destruction	price directive	tax exemption
art director	foot infection	sales convention	throat infection
band musician	gas explosion	sales discussion	tool assembly
bank deposit	health department	sales division	trade agreement
bank director	health suggestion	sales promotion	trade amendment
car mechanic	heart condition	speech improvement	trade convention
church attendance	house detective	sports announcer	train conductor
coin collector	mail delivery	stamp collector	train dispatcher
dance director	news announcement	steel production	wage agreement
farm equipment	news reporter	stock investment	wage proposal
field director	peace committee	store detective	wage reduction
fire department	price announcement	sweet potato	work agreement
fire insurance	price concession	tape recorder	work improvement
fire prevention	price consultant	tax attorney	work procedure
		tax consultant	work solution

List 22: ˙ ′ ˙ ⁻

accounting course	construction bond	mosquito bite	reduction gear
amusement park	construction gang	opinion poll	reflecting pool
apartment house	debating team	papaya juice	resistance coil
appliance store	delivery boy	petunia plant	retirement age
appointment book	delivery truck	phonetics course	retirement group
assembly line	department head	piano store	retirement plan
assembly plant	department store	piano wire	spaghetti sauce
banana crop	departure time	potato chips	suggestion box
banana leaf	discussion group	potato flakes	surveyor's rod
banana oil	dividing line	production chief	surveyor's tool
banana plant	division chief	production cost	tobacco crop
banana port	division head	production head	tobacco pouch
banana skin	election year	production line	tobacco smoke
banana stem	engagement ring	propeller shaft	tobacco tax
collection plate	induction coil	reception desk	tomato juice
committee room	invasion force	reception room	tomato plant
connecting rod	investment stock	recording booth	

List 23:   Noun Compounds—Longer Forms with Primary Stress on First Element

airconditioning unit	cotton picking machine	handwriting expert
airplane pilot	department store manager	headache powder
amusement park ride	drugstore clerk	lighthouse keeper
apartment house manager	election year results	lunchroom counter
armchair cover	fingernail polish	newspaper office
assembly line production	fire prevention day	notebook cover
basketball player	football field	out-patient clinic
beauty shop operator	fruit juice container	parking lot attendant
bookstore owner	furniture company president	passport division
chewing gum wrapper	gas station attendant	ping-pong table
coal mine operator	grocery store owner	postage stamp dispenser
construction gang head	handball court	post office department

railroad train
rocket launching device
roller skating rink
seashore development
shoeshine kit
shoe store manager

spaceship pilot
speech improvement class
steel production data
steering wheel mechanism
stock market forecast
streetcar conductor

sweetpotato vine
textbook division
toy store owner
trade agreement pact
typewriter table
volleyball court
wage reduction announcement

List 24:   Verb Compounds with Primary Stress on the First Element

air-condition	bootleg	downgrade	handcuff	lip-read	square dance
backbite	brainwash	dry-clean	hemstitch	mothproof	two-step
backhand	browbeat	eavesdrop	highlight	see-saw	typewrite
backslide	court-martial	fingerprint	hitchhike	sidestep	upgrade
backstop	crisscross	fireproof	horsewhip	sight-read	waterproof
backtrack	deadhead	footnote	housebreak	sight-see	whitewash
blackball	deadlock	fox-trot	ice-skate	sleepwalk	window-shop
blackmail	dovetail	ghostwrite	kidnap		

List 25:   Adjective Compounds with Primary Stress on the First Element

airborne	clockwise	footloose	hair-raising	inbred	mothproof
air-cooled	color-blind	footsore	handwritten	king-sized	nearsighted
airsick	cross-eyed	foremost	headlong	knock-kneed	one-eyed
armor-clad	crosswise	forthright	headstrong	law-abiding	pigeon-toed
armweary	die-hard	freeborn	heartbreaking	life-giving	pockmarked
backbreaking	dog-eared	freehand	heartbroken	lifelike	rainproof
bareback	dovetailed	free-lance	heartrending	lifelong	seasick
barefoot	drought-stricken	full-blooded	heartsick	lifesaving	snowbound
bloodshot	dumb struck	gaslit	heartwarming	life-sized	treelined
boldface	farsighted	ghostlike	hidebound	lightproof	typewritten
breakneck	fireproof	goosenecked	high-hat	lovelorn	waterproof
bullheaded	flea-bitten	grief-stricken	homesick	love-sick	weatherproof
carefree	flower-shaped	gunslinging	homespun	moonstruck	wholesale
childlike	foolhardy	hairlike	icebound	moss-grown	windblown
				moth-eaten	windswept

KEY TO EXERCISES

The answers given here to the various exercises in the book are based on the accompanying tapes.
Part 1 (page 11)

Exercise 1:

1.	angry		
2.		above	
3.			professor
4.		belief	
5.			decided
6.	wanted		
7.	movie		
8.		hotel	
9.		enjoy	
10.			example
11.			remembered
12.	people		
13.		forget	
4.		because	
15.	roses		

Exercise 2: The one that is different is *gentleman*.

Exercise 3: Yes. All the words have the same stress pattern.

120

Exercise 4:

	Same	Different
1. refer reefer		X
2. table pencil	X	
3. professor architect		X
4. accept accent		X
5. comforting exciting		X
6. amusing important	X	
7. winter weather	X	

Exercise 5:

1. (mon)ey
2. per(haps)
3. se(lec)tion
4. (tem)per-a-ture
5. (af)ter
6. per(mit)
7. em(ploy)-ment
8. (mar)vel-ous
9. (mod)ern
10. (per)ish-a-ble
11. con(tin)-ue
12. in(dus)trial
13. (hap)pi-ly
14. be(cause)
15. (for)tu-nate-ly
16. (noth)ing
17. a(mus)ing
18. (pos)si-bly
19. de(ter)
20. con(clu)sion

Part 2 (page 16)

Exercise 1:

	first syllable	*second syllable*	*third syllable*
1.			understánd
2.		northéastern	
3.	télephone		
4.	líbrary		
5.			seventéen
6.		inféction	
7.	hémisphere		
8.	émphasis		
9.	múltiply		
10.		idéa	

	first syllable	*second syllable*	*third syllable*
11.			introdúce
12.	réalize		
13.			disbelíeve
14.	télevise		
15.		unféeling	

Exercise 2: The word that is different is *disregard*.

Exercise 3:

1. con-ven-ient
2. ap-pre-ci-at-ed
3. or-ches-tra
4. pro-nun-ci-a-tion
5. in-dus-tri-ous
6. prin-ci-pal
7. rec-re-a-tion
8. op-por-tu-ni-ty
9. six-teen
10. im-ag-i-na-tion
11. stim-u-lat-ing
12. rev-o-lu-tion-ized
13. re-mark-a-bly
14. six-ty
15. per-fect-ly

Exercise 4:

		Same	Different
1.	machine picture		X
2.	telephone understand		X
3.	dictionary television	X	
4.	above early		X
5.	diplomat engineer		X
6.	forty fourteen		X
7.	coming working	X	
8.	telephone operate	X	
9.	emphasizes exercises	X	
10.	ago above	X	
11.	arriving department	X	
12.	understand diplomat		X

	Same	Different
13. calendar remember		X
14. Africa Alaska		X
15. result machine	X	
16. obey study		X
17. information necessary		X
18. weather summer	X	
19. mistake error		X
20. material experience	X	
21. telephone televise	X	
22. animal direction		X
23. experience information		X
24. electrician electrical		X
25. mechanical mechanizes		X

Part 3 (page 24)

Exercise 1: The two that are not noun compounds are 6. red shoes, 9. wool suit.

Exercise 2: No key.

Exercise 3: 1. enginéer   2. políce car   3. cándy   4. bárbershop
5. umbrélla   6. Japán   7. clássroom   8. wáter glass
9. ánimal   10. fíre prevention   11. éxercise
12. bús driver   13. Spánish   14. súitcoat   15. appréciate
16. síxty   17. táblecloth   18. machíne   19 sixtéen
20. néws reporter   21. educátion   22. fúrniture company
23. emplóyment   24. electrícity   25. óffice manager

Exercise 4: No key.

Exercise 5·

1. grocery store   2. bowling ball   3. mailman   4. butter knife
5. raincoat   6. candy store   7. furniture factory
8. drinking water   9. wrapping paper   10. farm equipment
11. postage stamp   12. movie theater   13. bread box
14. coffee pot   15. passenger train   16. repair man
17. cable car   18. garage mechanic   19. tomato juice
20. vegetable garden

Part 5 (page 39)

Exercise: 1. A,   2. B,   3. B,   4. B,   5. A,   6. B,   7. A,   8. A,   9. B,   10. A,
          11. B,   12. A,   13. B,   14. A,   15. B,   16. B,   17. B,   18. A,   19. B,   20. A.

Part 6 (page 55)

	Column 1	Column 2
1. I don't know Mr. Jones.	X	
2. John doesn't remember, Helen.		X
3. I haven't written, Mother.		X
4. She hasn't called Mary.	X	
5. I couldn't hear Dr. Jones.	X	
6. We haven't met, Miss Smith.		X
7. I haven't forgotten, Professor Johnson.		X
8. I haven't heard, Bill.		X
9. He doesn't remember Miss Black.	X	
10. We don't know, Dr. Smith.		X

Part 6 (page 58)

Exercise

	Column 1	Column 2
1. Do you remember Bill?	X	
2. Will you write, Mother?		X
3. Have you forgotten, Miss Smith?		X
4. Did you understand John?	X	
5. Do you remember Dr. Holmes?	X	
6. Do you know, Miss Nelson?		X
7. Can you hear Helen?	X	
8. Did you call, Mary?		X
9. Will you help, Jeff?		X
10. Have we met Mrs. Brown?	X	

Part 10 (page 93)

Exercise

1. émphasis   emphátic
2. hémisphere   hemisphérical
3. introdúce   introdúction
4. pérfect   pérfectly
5. condítion   condítioning
6. índustry   indústrious
7. appréciate   appreciátion
8. lúcky   lúckily
9. imágine   imaginátion
10. imágine   imáginative
11. conclúde   conclúsion
12. conclúde   conclúsive
13. válid   validíty